C000178351

A SIGNAL HONOUR

"To serve with men like these was a
signal honour indeed"

A SIGNAL HONOUR

With the Chindits
and
XIV Army in Burma

by

ROBIN PAINTER

LEO COOPER

First published in Great Britain 1999 by
Leo Cooper
an imprint of
Pen & Sword Books
47 Church Street
Barnsley
South Yorkshire
S70 2AS

ISBN 0 85052 707 4
Copyright © Robin Painter 1999

A CIP record for this book is
available from the British Library.

Typeset in 11/13pt Sabon by
Phoenix Typesetting, Ilkley, West Yorkshire

Printed in England by Redwood Books Ltd,
Trowbridge, Wilts

CONTENTS

DEDICATION

For MIN-P, my "M", who has sustained me through all the years since my time in Burma. A soldier's wife who followed the drum, she was known as "Flower" to the wives of many of my soldiers and deserves so much more from the Army than the meagre one-third of my pension to which she would be entitled should I die before her.

FOREWORD
BY
MAJOR GENERAL D.R. HORSFIELD OBE

A special relationship often develops between those in charge of training Officer Cadets and the eager young men embarking on a military career, whether this be in time of peace or the conscripted service of wartime. I had the good fortune to train Officer Cadets in wartime in Mhow in Central India and in peacetime at the Royal Military Academy, Sandhurst. This has provided me with long-term friendships, many with people in high places in Britain, India, Pakistan, Jordan and Sri Lanka.

Robin Painter was one of the first of this group, arriving at Mhow in 1942. He was an outstanding Cadet, passing out top of his course, an achievement which projected him immediately into a most difficult assignment which he did well to survive. He and I met from time to time during the years of our service and were brought close together as a team to provide the author, Philip Warner, with material for *The Vital Link, The Story of Royal Signals*, published in 1988.

It may have been this experience in the book world which gave Robin Painter the idea that he had good material of his own for a story, and an excellent story it is. In the few years from his schooldays to the end of his service in Burma he had marvellous variety of experience. Above all it illustrates how a young officer, still in his 'teens, found himself in totally strange circumstances of geography, language, removal from military support and separation from any superiors – and survived. It also highlights the severe threat from debilitating and life-threatening illness which was all part of the Burma war.

Formal training provided little assistance in the circumstances he faced, particularly as he missed the preparatory training given to the majority of the Wingate troops. He was thrown back on his own resources in what a Pakistan General, in different circumstances, described to me as cave man soldiering.

Wars often produce the unexpected. This book illustrates for young and old the excitement or worse of recognizing imminent disaster and the satisfaction of delivering oneself and one's soldiers from the apparent jaws of death.

David Hornsfeld

ACKNOWLEDGEMENTS

Many friends and old comrades have given me invaluable support and encouragement in the preparation of this personal narrative. To them all I give my sincere thanks. In particular, I am most grateful to those who have read the manuscript, both chapter by chapter and as a complete book, giving me advice and constructive criticism as the story poured out of me from memory and from notes made at the time.

Philip Warner, a firm friend and colleague, gave guidance and encouragement which kept me going. Having been a prisoner-of-war and "slave labourer", first on the BANGKOK to MOULMEIN "railway of death" and later in the copper mines of Japan, his intimate knowledge of the obscene brutality and ruthlessness of the Japanese enabled him to identify completely with my story. His talents and experience as an author specializing in military history, coupled with this knowledge of the Japanese as an enemy, gave me access to advice of the highest quality. I cannot thank him enough.

To Major General David Horsfield I owe a debt which I can never repay. We first met in 1942 when he taught me the rudiments of the "craft" of being an officer – he had just fought his way out of Burma during the terrible first retreat but never mentioned it to us, whereas some lesser men would have seized the opportunity to "shoot a line" of massive proportions to the officer cadets in their charge. His teaching on leadership was impeccable and completely relevant to my later experience. Without realizing it at the time, we later fought close to one another during the Imphal siege, he with 23 Indian Division and

I with 20 Indian Division. He has given me unstinting help in the preparation of my narrative and I am proud to have known him.

My special thanks go to Colonel Archie Pagan and Colonel John West, with both of whom I have had the privilege and pleasure to serve and who have taken great care to read and comment on my manuscript.

Perhaps my greatest expression of gratitude is due to Jan Nicholson (now Mrs P.J. Cornick), then the Archivist at the Royal Signals Museum at Blandford Camp, Dorset. Without her help my manuscript could not have been completed. Her patience, understanding, tolerance and efficiency are beyond praise. Every word of my hand-written manuscript became a neatly presented typescript from her word processor, free of error and at remarkable speed. She introduced modifications, alterations and rearrangements "at the drop of a hat", with a smile and without complaint, often suggesting rewording which was entirely appropriate. I believe she looks upon my narrative as "her book" as much as it is my story. I am deeply grateful to her.

The quotation from *The Road Past Mandalay*, page 165, is reproduced by kind permission of Laurence Pollinger Limited and the Estate of John Masters.

I am also grateful to the Imperial War Museum for permission to reproduce illustrations from their collection.

Lastly my thanks go to my dear sister Patricia de Brabant and her husband Jack, a brave man who, in 1940, decided without hesitation to continue to fight against the Nazis, after his own country had been overrun and occupied by the enemy. They both read my narrative chapter by chapter as each was completed, and their comments and encouraging letters were a great help.

ROBIN PAINTER
POOLE, DORSET
1999

PREFACE

This is a story of growing up.

> – of learning how to kill and then of killing;

> – of learning how to signal and then of signalling;

> – of learning how to lead and then of leading;

> and of learning how to survive and then – by some miracle of good fortune – of surviving.

It is also a story of comradeship.

It is a personal narrative.

The story I have written is not unique. On the contrary, most of the experiences I have described are similar to those of many thousands of other young men who were caught up in the war against the Japanese in Burma in 1943, 1944 and 1945. I hope that some of those who survived may read this and remember.

Much of what I have written started as notes made soon after the events described. To write the whole story has been, for me, akin to the release of a safety valve when the pressure within me became too great to withstand. During the three-year period of the Second World War from 1943 to 1945, I spent much of my time on active service in Burma and the horror of total war helped me to grow from teenage to manhood at a much accelerated pace. It also helped me to decide to serve for 31 years as a permanent regular commissioned officer in the British Army in the hope that, however small my personal contribution might be and believing in the principle of the deterrent, I could spend a large part of my working life doing something to help prevent a recurrence of this horror. Knowing the nature of man, perhaps this was a sublime hope.

Another factor was, of course, the comradeship I had found during those years in Burma. I learned again and again the true worth of men in situations of extreme adversity. The Indian soldiers, whether they were Punjabi Musselmen, Madrassis, Sikhs, or from Rajputana, the North West Frontier or elsewhere, were superb. They were all volunteers and were prepared to fight – and to die – for *our* cause, with loyalty, devotion to duty and extraordinary courage. So it was also with the Gurkhas from Nepal, the bravest of the brave. In Burma we also had West Africans and East Africans, far from home, who fought for us with similar loyalty and courage. I learned to have deep respect and affection for the hill tribesmen of Manipur and Upper Burma – the Nagas, the Chins and especially the Karens and Kachins – so many of whom suffered torture and death from the Japanese, giving their lives for *us*.

This was predominantly an infantry war, fought and won more by the foot soldiers of infantry battalions than by any of the rest of us; but no matter what branch of the Army, we were all very closely involved and engaged with the enemy, by the very nature of the conflict and the country. The jungle does not permit any of the elements of an Army to have preferential treatment or an easier time than others. The threat from the enemy was around all of us for most of the time.

Perhaps for me the most important lesson learnt was to discover the true worth of that indomitable human being, the British soldier. He will grumble about things that don't matter, especially on those rare occasions when life is easy for him, but will accept and put up with indescribable conditions and situations without a murmur when the going gets really hard. He will fight like a tiger for himself and his comrades, but will not put up with bullying and cannot stand the devious, the pretentious or the over-bearing. He has to be well led and never driven. The worse the situation or the conditions become, the more his special sort of humour becomes apparent. He is one of those rare human beings who can laugh at himself. He can be extremely tough and hard-bitten and yet be reduced to tears if, for example, his mule has been wounded and has to be "put down". As an all-round professional soldier, I do not believe there is any better in the world.

At an early stage in the campaign in Burma, I was to learn the complete relevance of the sound advice about leadership that was given to us by the instructors at the Royal Signals Officer Cadet Training Unit (OCTU) at Mhow. Many young subalterns, when confronted for the first time by soldiers placed under their command, supervision or responsibility, tend to look upon these men as though somehow they are in conflict with them. This is probably because of insecurity, uncertainty and lack of confidence on the part of the young and inexperienced officer (some bad officers never fully free themselves of this attitude towards their subordinates). His solution is sometimes to assume an arrogant and aggressive approach to his men and this can be fatal, particularly in war. The advice I was given (and which I soon found to be fundamental to good leadership) included a reminder that:

"Your own soldiers and subordinates are your *friends* and *comrades* – there are plenty of enemies around in war, so do not add to them by treating your friends as enemies. In addition, it is essential to realize and accept that your subordinates may well know much more about their own particular area of expertise than you do. Accept this and respect them for it and in turn you will earn their respect. Pretend that you know much more than you actually do and you will soon be found out, at the expense of their respect for you. Work *with* them, not as a dominant bully but as a firm, decisive 'guiding hand'; and always be ready and eager to learn. All this can and should be achieved without any loss of discipline. Do not attempt to 'curry favour' by being soft with them but do everything you can to look after their interests. Above all, remember that your own soldiers are your friends, who may well make all the difference between survival or death for you and for them. If you *do* work with and for them and not against them, both you and they will reap the benefit and your unit or sub-unit will be well on the way to being a happy one in addition to developing the efficiency that will be vital to success."

So spoke the sages at Mhow OCTU – and how right they were.

The long campaign in Burma was a dirty war. It received little publicity and has never been as familiar to the people of the "home country" as have other campaigns of the Second World War. For the sake of all those many thousands of Commonwealth soldiers, sailors and airmen who took part but did not survive, I hope this small narrative of mine will help in some measure to remind us of their sacrifice and to be thankful.

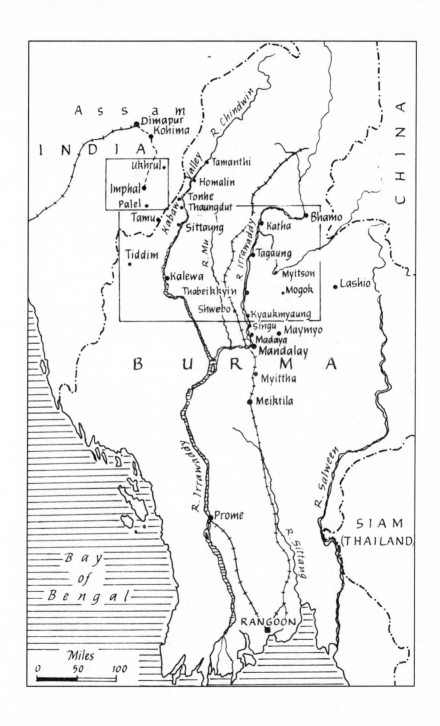

A S S A M

Dimapur
Kohima

I N D I A

Ukhrul

Imphal
Palel

Tamu

Tiddim

R. Chindwin

Tamanthi

Homalin

Tonhe
Thaungdut

Sittaung

Kalewa

Thabeikkyin

Shwebo

Katha

Tagaung

Myitson
Mogok

Lashio

Bhamo

C H I N A

Kabaw Valley

R. Mu

R. Irrawaddy

Kyaukmyaung

Singu   Maymyo
Madaya
Mandalay

B   U   R   M   A

Myittha

Meiktila

R. Irrawaddy

R. Salween

R. Sittang

Prome

S I A M
(THAILAND)

B a y
of
B e n g a l

RANGOON

Miles
0   50   100

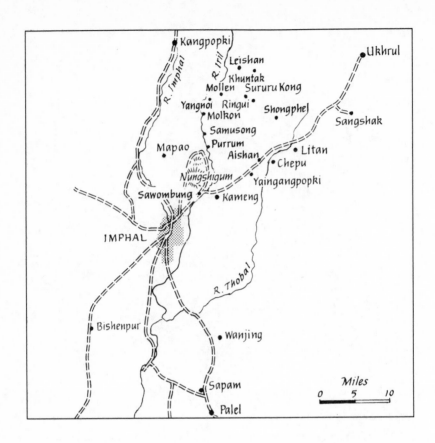

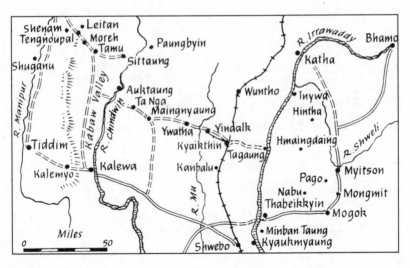

PRONUNCIATION OF SOME
BURMESE PLACE NAMES

AUKTAUNG	OAK-TONG
INYWA	IN-YOU-ARE
KALEMYO	KAL-AY-ME-OH
KALEWA	KAL-AY-WAH
KATHA	CATARRH
KYAIKTHIN	CHAIK-TIN
KYAUKMYAUNG	CHOKE-ME-YONG
MAINGNYAUNG	MAN-YONG
MAN NA	MUN-NAR
MOGOK	MOW-GOK
MYITKINA	MITCH-IN-ARH
MYITSON	MITS-ON
PAUNGBYIN	PONG-BIN
PINLEBU	PIN-LAY-BOO
SHENAM	SHEN-ARM
TAGAUNG	TAR-GONG
TA NGA	TAR-UN-GAR
TENGNOUPAL	TENG-NOO-PARL
UKHRUL	YOU-CRUEL
YENATHA	YEN-ARTHUR
YE-U	YAY-OO

INTRODUCTION

The story I have to tell in this personal narrative centres on the long campaign against the Japanese in Burma. I was totally involved on active service in this campaign for four months in early 1943, for the whole of 1944 and for the first three months of 1945. The remainder of my story is concerned with training and preparation for these periods in action against a vicious enemy, with rare and brief breaks away from the fighting and with my final departure from Burma and return to England when, for me, it was all over.

Since Burma is the essential centre-piece, it might be helpful to the reader if I attempt to describe some of the salient features of this relatively unknown country. Those who are already familiar with this land of contrasts and extremes will perhaps be patient with me and forgive my inevitable errors and omissions.

First it should be said that there are large areas of Burma which are extremely unpleasant, being disease-filled, hot and dusty in the dry season and steaming hot and wet in the monsoons. Chaungs, which in the dry season are dried-up river beds or at most just tiny streams, become swollen to impassable raging torrents in the monsoons. Land which was fought over during the rainy season often became a morass of mud and shell holes reminiscent of the battlefields of Flanders in the First World War. Much of the country is covered with thick jungle, which, particularly in the monsoon season, abounds with leeches and other small unpleasant creatures which delight in attaching themselves to the human body. The bacteria and amoebae of dysentery are ever present. Malarial mosquitoes abound and, in some areas, the typhus tick is rampant. Yet there are also parts of the country where it is a joy to be, usually only at the best times of the year. Such places are, in the main, high in the hills and mountains. Maymyo in the Shan States is a typical example.

Somehow I always found myself on what was known as the "Central Front". As a consequence I became familiar with the country around Imphal, through Nagaland and down into the Kabaw Valley, which runs parallel to the River Chindwin but some 20 miles west of it; with the River Chindwin itself and eastwards from it to the "railway corridor" and the River Irrawaddy, and further eastwards across the Irrawaddy to the River Shweli and onwards through the Kachin Hills and into the Yunnan Province of China; also southwards down the east bank of the River Irrawaddy as far as Mandalay and southeastwards through the Shan States to Maymyo. I did not go to the far north of Burma nor to the country south of Mandalay towards Rangoon. Hence my intimate knowledge of the country is limited to Central Burma and the southern part of Upper Burma, and to those parts of the country which border on to Manipur State in the west and the Yunnan Province of China in the east.

Burma can be described in simplified fashion as a country which consists of a central plain, surrounded by mountains in the shape of a horseshoe around that plain and with the sea (the Bay of Bengal and the Andaman Sea) to the south, forming the open base of the inverted horseshoe. This is perhaps a description which is too simplified, as there are hills and escarpments rising from the central plain. The people who inhabit the surrounding mountains and hills are quite different from those who inhabit the central plain. The former are hill tribes. (Chins, Nagas, Karens, Kachins, Shans etc) while the latter are true Burmese. The hill tribes were in general pro-British, whereas the Burmese of the central plain were often anti-British, pro-Japanese or willing to serve either according to their best advantage.

The economy of the country depended to a great extent on the natural communications provided by three major rivers, all flowing from north to south. The first and most important of these was the River Irrawaddy, navigable by river steamer from as far north as Myitkyina, all the way to the delta of the river where it enters the Andaman Sea near Rangoon. The second in importance was the River Chindwin, the largest and most important tributary of the Irrawaddy, joining it near to Myingyan and about 60 miles west of Mandalay. The Chindwin rose in the mountains to the north-east of Ledo and ran from north to south close to the border with India until it reached the confluence with the Irrawaddy. For the period from Mid-1942, when the Japanese advance across Burma came to a halt because of over-extended lines of communication and the coming of the monsoons, to March 1944, when the Japanese began their major offensive on Imphal and Kohima, the River Chindwin could be regarded as the "dividing line" separating the Japanese and Allied forces on the "Central Front". The third major river was the Salween, which flows from north to south down the eastern side of the country, for the most part between Burma and China (Yunnan Province) and, further south, between Burma and Siam (Thailand), until it flows into the Andaman Sea at Moulmein. Midway between the lower reaches of the Rivers Irrawaddy and Salween, and following for a while the valley of the smaller River Sittang, a main line railway ran from Rangoon through Pegu and northwards to Mandalay, from where it continued further northwards up the "railway corridor", running to the west of and parallel to the River Irrawaddy until it reached Myitkyina in the far north. From this main railway line there were other short branch lines to east and west, to serve a few of the more important localities but, as with the main rivers, the predominant movement trend and requirement was between the south, the centre and the north of the country. In normal times the only practical way into or out of Burma was through the sea ports in the south. Because of the extreme difficulties presented by mountains, river barriers and disease-filled jungle terrain, no roads existed between India and Burma. Between the east of the country and China, the "Burma Road" had been built through the mountains from Mandalay through Maymyo, Lashio, Wanting, Longling, Baoshan and onwards to Kunming. The original purpose of this road was to enable the Allies to send material aid by lorry convoys from the coastal port of Rangoon to the Chinese Army of Chiang Kai-Shek, fighting the Japanese inside China. With the fall of Rangoon and then the whole of Burma to the Japanese Army in the first five months of 1942, the so-called "Burma Road" could not be used for this purpose as it was in the hands of the enemy. From then on, the only means available to the Allies to transport war material into Yunnan Province was by cargo carrying aircraft from India "over the Hump" and into China.

In addition to the "Central Front", there were two other major battle zones on the India-Burma border during the period from late 1942 to 1945. In the far north American-led Chinese troops under General "Vinegar Joe" Stilwell fought their way slowly eastwards from Ledo towards Myitkyina, building behind them a new "Burma Road" which was intended to reach China and replace the original and now useless "Burma Road" held by the enemy. This new road was never completed but some extremely hard fighting (not only by Chinese but also by British Chindits from the 1944 "Second Wingate" expedition) was involved until Myitkyina was eventually recaptured in August 1944. The other major battle zone was in the Arakan, where the extreme south-west of Burma joined the shore line of India, facing the Bay of Bengal to the south of Chittagong. The mountains of the Arakan Yomas ran south from the Chin Hills almost to the coast at Akyab and were virtually impassable for major land operations. As a consequence, action between the Allied Army and the Japanese took place for the most part in a narrow, swampy and unhealthy strip of land between the shore line and the mountain ranges. The Japanese tried on several occasions to invade India by this route but, although some of the bitterest fighting of the campaign was involved, the Arakan was considered by the enemy High Command to be something of a "side show". Their major attacks in the Arakan were used on several occasions to draw reserves away from the "Central Front", where the Japanese had decided to concentrate their main effort by taking Imphal and then invading India through Assam.

For much of the period from June 1942 until July/August 1944 Imphal was the main base for Allied operations on the "Central Front". After the disastrous retreat of the Allied Army from Burma into India during the first five months of 1942 (a defeat described by the anglophobe General Stilwell of the US Army as "a hell of a licking"), the Imphal Plain and surrounding territory down to the River Chindwin, into the Kabaw Valley and south to Tiddim in the Chin Hills, was defended by two veteran Indian Divisions. These were 17 Indian Division in the Tiddim area and 23 Indian Division down in the Kabaw Valley in the area of Moreh and Tamu. These two Divisions were later joined by 20 Indian Division, which took over in the Tamu area to enable 23 Division to withdraw to the Imphal Plain for a rest. Still later, these three Indian Divisions were joined by 50 Indian Parachute Brigade, which was moved to a position near Sangshak on the Ukhrul track to the north-east of the Imphal Plain to cover the possible approaches to the Plain from the River Chindwin by this route. This whole force of three Indian Divisions and one Indian Parachute Brigade made up IV Corps, under the command of Lieutenant General Geoffrey Scoones, and was responsible for the defence of the "Central Front", based on the Imphal Plain.

There was one very significant disadvantage to the choice of Imphal as the main base for operations in this area. It was a choice to which there was no alternative as there was no other suitable route from India (and a railhead) through the mountains and down to the River Chindwin. The "Line of Communications" (L of C) was the only major "doorway" between Burma and India on the "Central Front" and had to be defended. The serious disadvantage was that the road from the railhead at Dimapur, through Kohima to the Imphal Plain, ran from north to south by the only possible route through the Naga Hills and thus ran almost parallel to the River Chindwin, which was some 60 miles away to the east of the road. Hence the basic and most important principle of never having an L of C which ran parallel to the "Front Line" – in this case the River Chindwin – had to be put to one side. The only reassurance was that the country between the Chindwin and the road consisted of the Naga Hill Tracts. These were composed of a seemingly endless series of steep hills and ridges, with deep valleys between and with thick jungle covering the whole area, and were optimistically assumed to be virtually impenetrable for enemy forces in sufficient strength to move across and undertake a major offensive. When, in March/April 1944, the road was cut at Kohima and elsewhere and the Imphal Plain was surrounded by the Japanese and cut off from the outside world except from the air, the error of this optimistic assumption became evident. In fact and in spite of this, the victory of the Indian and British Divisions at Imphal and Kohima in 1944, and the resultant decimation of more than three Japanese Divisions, proved to be the turning point of the war in Burma with as much significance in that campaign as the Allied victory at Alamein had in the campaign in North Africa.

Throughout this narrative frequent mention has been made of the "jungle". This word has a very wide and diverse meaning, as there are so many different types of jungle to be encountered in Burma. Sometimes we had to deal with thick, tangled vegetation through which a way had to be hacked by brute force and where the sky was rarely seen. Sometimes our movement was through open teak forest, easy to traverse and a welcome change permitting trouble-free marching conditions at night. The disadvantage was the noise made by marching feet on the carpet of brittle dry leaves, which could be heard at a considerable distance. There were times when we encountered thick clumps of elephant grass rising to heights of well over six feet and which could rip clothes and scratch flesh as we forced our way through it. Another unpleasant hazard was swamp jungle. Perhaps forcing a path through thick bamboo was one of the most difficult tasks to tackle. A major enemy in the monsoons was the mud and the slippery slopes of narrow paths up and down steep hillsides, especially if one was following where others had gone before. During Operation "Longcloth" – the "First Wingate" expedition in 1943 – we used footpaths and tracks with great caution and only when our advanced patrols (usually men of our Burma Rifles) had reported the way clear of the enemy ahead of us. As we were passing through Japanese-held territory for the whole of that operation, ambushes or accidental encounters with the enemy were a constant hazard. We often moved at night, but there were times when cross-country movement through dense jungle made this impossible. The combination of steep hills and thick jungle sometimes almost overcame us. I remember particularly the difficulties of crossing the Zibyu Hills to reach the escarpment overlooking the valley of the River Mu and also the agony of marching through the Kodaung Hill Tracts on the way out to China in 1943. Yet the jungle in all its various forms could be a friend and an ally for, given good jungle discipline and control, concealment became easy and again and again the enemy could pass nearby without realizing our presence.

This then is the background to my narrative. Burma is not a country for which I developed an affection but my feelings of respect, gratitude and admiration for the people of the hill tribes of that country have remained with me to this day.

Chapter 1

BEGINNINGS
STUDENT TO SOLDIER 1939–41

We came down from Mount Cinto and into Calvi on 4 September 1939. There was pandemonium in the town and we soon learned that both France and Great Britain were at war with Germany. We had known nothing of this on 3 September, as we were still on the mountain when the war actually started. In Calvi the chaos resulted from cancellation of all ferries between Corsica and the mainland and the consequences of general mobilization. The order for all French Army reservists was to report to the nearest barracks. As a result the barracks in Calvi, at that time occupied by a regular battalion of Senegalese troops, was quickly overwhelmed by the flood of reservists, many of whom were in Corsica on holiday. As no ferries were running, these men could not get to Marseilles or Cannes and therefore fulfilled their obligation as reservists by reporting at the gates of the barracks.

We too were in difficulties. Our month of touring Corsica on bicycles, camping each night as we explored the island, had come to an end. We had run out of money and our return tickets to Marseilles by ferry were useless until the ferry services started again. Meanwhile we had to eat. As "*Eclaireurs de France*" (the French equivalent of Rover Scouts) our leader, a man aged about 30 and a Grenoblois, persuaded the authorities at the barracks to let us work as "kitchen helps" for the sudden flood of reservists. In return for potato peeling and kitchen chores such as cleaning cooking pots and scrubbing the floors, all eighteen

1

of us were fed and allowed to "bed down" in the corridors of the cookhouse block. We existed in this way for almost two weeks until, at last, the ferries started running again and we were able to begin our return journey by ferry from Calvi to Marseilles and thence by train to Grenoble.

All this had begun in the Spring of 1939, when I left England for Grenoble, Isére, in that corner of south-east France where once, more than a century before, Napoleon had successfully confronted those who had been sent to arrest him after his escape from Elba. Near the town, at a village called Laffrey, he had talked his way out of a tricky situation and persuaded the soldiers who were his would-be captors to join him for the "Hundred Days" which ended on the battlefield of Waterloo.

I went to France as a student at the Université de Grenoble, to improve my spoken French and to learn something of the literature of the country. While studying at Grenoble – and I was 16 years old when I arrived there – I stayed *en famille* with Madame Chabert and her son Marc, who lived in a delightful little house at 81 bis Avenue des Bains. Madame Chabert treated me as her son and Marc, who was my age, became a firm friend. He was to die as a member of the "Resistance" later in the war. No English was spoken by the family and perhaps my colloquial French benefited more from this situation than from my studies at the University. My course progressed without incident and it was a happy time, for we were too young as yet to realize the full implication of the dark shadows that were gathering to warn the world of the holocaust to come.

Staying with us at 81 bis were two young German students, a boy and a girl who were also following courses at the University. They too became good friends and we were a happy family together. Madame Chabert, big, round and maternal, was an excellent cook and I have never forgotten the enormous meals presented to us each day. At Grenoble the Spring and Summer of 1939 seemed perfect, the sun shone every day – for one forgets the occasional rain shower – and we worked and played and no doubt did things we should not have done with the careless acceptance and abandon of youth.

As the summer days passed we remained oblivious of the gathering storm. One day in late July our two German friends packed and left Grenoble quite suddenly. No explanation was given. One day they were there, the next they had gone. We thought little of it and were just sad about their departure because we had liked them well enough and could not understand why they had not even said goodbye to us.

By early August arrangements had been completed for Marc Chabert and myself to join a party of eighteen *Eclaireurs de France* for a camping and cycling holiday in Corsica. We planned to be away from Grenoble for four weeks and to tour the whole island in that time. On 3 August we left Grenoble by train for Lyons, where we boarded the Paris–Marseilles express. Our bicycles were to be hired on arrival at Ajaccio and we carried with us only our rucksacks, with small tents, cooking gear and other camping paraphernalia distributed between us. We arrived in Marseilles in the evening of the same day and there boarded the night ferry for Ajaccio. Arrangements were fairly basic and we slept as best we could on the open deck of the ferry, arriving on the island in the early hours of the next morning. The leader of our party soon had us eating breakfast in a dingy café near to the docks. The place was obviously known to him from previous visits, for the proprietor was most hospitable and we were able to leave our kit in a small room at the back of the café while we explored the town during the morning. We negotiated the hire of bicycles to cover our stay for the next four weeks (as we were booked to return to the mainland from Calvi, arrangements were made to leave the bicycles at a cycle shop there) and we had an enjoyable time in the main food market, where we bought provisions enough to last us for the next few days. That night we stayed in Ajaccio, sleeping on the floor of the café at the invitation of our new-found friend, but we were so tired by this time that the shelter and food were welcome and we slept well. We had visited the birthplace of Napoleon and had thoroughly explored the capital of Corsica during this first day on the island.

Early next morning we set off by bicycle and during the next three weeks we made our way through Sartene to Bonifacio (that fascinating ancient walled town built on a cliff top overlooking the Straits between Corsica and Sardinia). We then moved up the east coast of the island through Porto Vecchio, Solenzara, Aleria,

3

Folelli and Bastia to Cap Corse in the far north, camping each night of our journey. From Cap Corse we turned west, along the north coast of the island, and travelled through St Florent and L'Ile Rousse to Calvi. From there we rode down to Porto, on the west coast just north of Ajaccio and so, by this time, had almost circumnavigated the whole island. We spent a few days at Porto, a beautiful spot where we rested and swam in the warm sea, and it was then decided that we should return to Calvi and go inland to climb Mount Cinto before starting our return journey to Grenoble. It was in this way that we found ourselves "employed" on a temporary basis as "kitchen helps" in the Senegalese barracks in Calvi, waiting for the resumption of ferry services to the mainland which had been cancelled (somewhat hysterically, we thought!) because the Second World War had started.

At last we were able to travel back to Grenoble. In Marseilles we found more scenes of pandemonium as "General Mobilization" proceeded apace. Our journey by train to Lyons, and onwards to Grenoble, was a nightmare of overcrowding as reservists moved to the reporting centres of their designated regiments. Travel by night was in complete darkness as "blackout" was being enforced and from Marseilles onwards every town was without street lighting. Eventually we arrived back safely at 81 bis Avenue des Bains, much to the relief of Madame Chabert, and I resumed my studies at the University.

In due course my father, a regular officer in the Royal Navy, must have decided that it was time for me to return to England. The instructions I received from him were quite precise and left no room for argument. I bade farewell to Madame Chabert and to Marc, her son, and started the long journey home through Paris and a "blacked out" France which by now was fully engaged in what became known as the "Phoney War". I crossed the Channel from Dieppe to Newhaven in a darkened ferry and was home in London for Christmas 1939.

In January 1940 and after discussion with my father during a short leave for Christmas – at that time he was doing a spell of "shore duty" and was the Naval Intelligence Officer based at Barry Docks in South Wales – I returned to my old school, University College School (UCS) in the Upper Sixth Form which specialized in preparation for entry examinations into the Armed Forces as a regular officer. My parents had a flat in north-west London, at Hampstead, only 10 minutes walk away from UCS, and I was to spend most of 1940 studying for the "Special Entry Examination" for entry into the Royal Navy. As I was short-sighted and had to wear spectacles, I was excluded from acceptance into the Executive Branch in which my father served and could only try for the Paymaster Branch. I was not very keen on this, but my father wanted me to have a career in the Royal Navy and so I went along with the idea and tried my best. Unfortunately, this was not good enough. I studied for more than a year, while momentous things were going on around me, but to no avail. The "Special Entry" was a competitive examination with an average of 500 candidates each time the examinations were held, of whom the top 25 were accepted. Of this 25, the top 5 (for some reason) were accepted as Paymaster Cadets. I sat the examination twice, once in the Autumn of 1940 and again in early 1941. Although on each occasion I did well in the "Interview" element of the examination (probably because I came from a "Naval" family), the nearest I came to the "select 5" at the top was 29th.

Throughout this period of my return to UCS, I had rejoined the Officer Training Corps (OTC) at the School. I had already held the rank of Sergeant in the OTC and had obtained my "Cert A" by the time I left the School to go to France. When in April/May 1940 the war started in earnest for Norway, Denmark, Holland, Belgium, France and ourselves – the Polish people, of course, had suffered defeat by the Nazis in September 1939 and this had brought us into the war – the lives of all of us changed dramatically. Following the fall of France in June 1940, and after the epic of Dunkirk, Great Britain stood alone against Nazi Germany. The Battle of Britain began and the Germans started the aerial bombardment of our towns, cities and defences. At this time, when invasion across the Channel seemed probable, one of the measures taken by Churchill was to order the formation of the "Local Defence Volunteers" (LDV) – later to become known as the "Home Guard". The vast majority of men who volunteered for the LDV were veterans of the First World War, too old to join the regular forces but not too old to come forward to help defend their homeland. There were also some who, as yet, were too young to join the regular forces but who were eager to make some contribution to the war effort. I was one of these and I found myself attending evening LDV parades three or four times each week, dressed in my OTC uniform with the three stripes of a Sergeant on my sleeves, taking men who were old enough to be my grandfather on drill parades and later, when at last we were issued with firearms, on weapon training. These elderly men, with so much experience of the horrors of war in the trenches 25 years earlier, were so keen and understanding that they relished being ordered about and taught by a young "pip-squeak" of 17 years, wearing khaki uniform with Sergeant's stripes on his arm. At first they wore civilian clothes with an armband with LDV printed on it. Rifle drill was with wooden pick handles until, to the delight of us all, issues of battledress and Lee-Enfield rifles materialized. At about the same time the designation "LDV" was dropped and we were all issued with shoulder titles to sew on our battledress, reading "Home Guard". On a roster system, some of us patrolled Hampstead Heath every night from dusk to dawn, looking for German paratroops who never arrived. We guarded key points considered to be likely sabotage targets and took our tasks very seriously. I really believe that, had the enemy appeared in our area, the Home Guard would have given a good account of themselves.

However, the only sign of the enemy was the constant bombing of London which we all experienced night after night throughout the summer, autumn and winter of 1940. Somehow everyone seemed to get used to the air raid sirens giving warning of approaching bombers, the exploding of the bombs, the noise of the anti-aircraft (AA) guns and of shrapnel from exploding AA shells whizzing through the air nearby, and then, at last, the sirens sounding the "All Clear". All this became a nightly routine and I suppose we all became somewhat fatalistic about our chances of "coming to grief" or surviving. I remember one particular night, when patrolling on Hampstead Heath, standing at the top of Parliament Hill and watching the whole of London's East End and dockland going up in flames – a never-to-be-forgotten sight. In spite of (or perhaps because of) all this,

6

the spirit of the people became almost magical. Everyone seemed prepared to help everyone else, class divisions began to disappear and a grim determination seemed to grip the nation, a determination not to give in but to defeat this upstart German dictator and his Nazi thugs. A spirit began to prevail the like of which I had not seen before and, sadly, I have not seen since, although, if similar circumstances were to occur again, I am sure the British people would show the same sort of reaction.

My home at this time was the flat in Canfield Gardens which consisted of the lower two floors of a house in a quiet road near to Swiss Cottage. My mother and sister Patricia spent the whole war living there, although my sister went away on "war work" for one or two long periods. We slept in bunks under the stairs on the lowest floor of the house. The stairs had been reinforced with stout timber beams and three bunks had been built into the space beneath to form an effective "air raid shelter". Unless the house received a direct hit, we felt reasonably secure from the bombing when sleeping there.

In August 1940 a small French cargo ship (8000 tons) called *Le Rhin* arrived at Barry Docks and came under my father's wing. Only six men of the ship's original crew had agreed to continue the struggle after the fall of France, the remainder having elected to return to France from Gibraltar, where the ship had been taken over by the Royal Navy. When it came under my father's control at Barry, the crew had been made up by French, Belgian and Polish volunteers who had escaped from France and who were determined to continue the fight against the Nazis. At Barry *Le Rhin* became the "Q" ship HMS *Fidelity* and was refitted and transformed into a fighting ship, while keeping its old outward appearance. It was later used on various dangerous missions which included dropping and picking up secret agents and "Resistance" personnel on the Mediterranean coast of France. The collection of officers on board consisted of three from the French Navy, a few from the French merchant navy and four Army officers – one French and three Belgians. They were vetted by Naval Intelligence and then introduced by my father to Commander Dunderdale, a mysterious figure based at the Admiralty in London who was responsible for certain highly secret Naval Intelligence activities.

They were then given *noms de guerre* (to protect their families left behind in occupied territory) and were accepted into the Royal Navy with regular commissions, but only for the duration of the war. The senior among them was a member of French Naval Intelligence named Claude Peri (also known as Claude Costa). He was a Corsican but became "Lieutenant Commander Jack Langlais" for the duration. He must have been one of the very few officers to be sentenced to death *in absentia* by the French Government and later to be awarded the Croix de Guerre with Palm. His second in command was Albert Guerrisse, whose *nom de guerre* was Pat O'Leary. He had been a medical officer in the Belgian Army and was to become the founder, organizer and operator of the famous "Pat Circuit", which helped more than 600 Allied aircrew, after being shot down, to escape across German occupied Belgium and France, avoiding capture and returning safely to the United Kingdom. He was eventually captured, tortured and imprisoned by the Gestapo and became one of the most decorated men in the Second World War, receiving the George Cross among many other awards. Another of this band of angry, determined and courageous young men, whose home countries had fallen into the hands of the Nazis, was a member of the Belgian Royal Family, a cavalry officer named Jack de Brabant. As his *nom de guerre* he became Lieutenant Commander Jack Ahern for the rest of the war. He also became my brother-in-law, marrying my sister Patricia. Most of this happy band visited our flat in Hampstead from time to time, at the invitation of my parents, when they came up to London either on duty visits to the Admiralty or "on pleasure bent". It was in this way that my sister met her future husband for the first time. Meanwhile my father was busily engaged at Barry in the business of creating a "Q" ship out of a somewhat battered tramp steamer. Sadly, after many successful missions, HMS *Fidelity* was torpedoed and lost with all hands off the Azores on 1 January 1943, when on passage to the Far East. Happily for us, neither my brother-in-law nor Pat O'Leary were on board at the time, being on other secret missions elsewhere.

As can be understood, all this exciting activity captured my imagination. I thought then that my facility with colloquial

French might get me a job as a deckhand on board one of the trawlers controlled by Dunderdale's organization and which were used to run agents across the Channel to France from time to time. All this sounded very romantic to me as a 17-year-old and I asked my father if he could put in a word for me. I heard nothing for many months and then, after I had joined the Army and had become an officer cadet, I received a letter forwarded from my father which summoned me to an interview, presumably to consider me for an appointment in Dunderdale's organization. I was able to telephone and explain that I now had other commitments. Looking back, I believe it was very fortunate that I just missed the possibility of a job with this most secret organization, because there would have been no future in it for me from the career point of view. It would most probably have been employment of a highly dangerous nature, with little or no reward for an eager and ambitious young man. I have often wondered what my attitude would have been had I known then what lay in store for me in Burma during the next four years.

In March 1941 my sister Patricia sailed in a small merchant ship in convoy to Halifax, Nova Scotia. She was one of a team of young British beauties chosen to promote exports of our *haute couture* garments to South America for the Board of Trade (at that time she was becoming one of the top mannequins of the London fashion houses). From Halifax they travelled by train to New York and from there by boat to South America. She was back in England again by September 1941, having travelled across the Atlantic in convoy from New York as one of only two passengers in a Dutch cargo boat.

28 May 1941 was my 18th birthday. My father was at sea again. He was born in 1897 and so was old enough to serve at sea throughout the First World War and yet was still young enough to serve at sea throughout the Second. In 1914 he was a Midshipman on board the old cruiser HMS *Minerva* in the Red Sea when war was declared. He now held the rank of Commander. His ship was the newly commissioned AA light cruiser HMS *Pozarica* and he was delighted with her. Soon after my birthday he arranged a short trip for me and I joined the ship at Milford Haven, where she was based. At that time HMS

Pozarica was escorting convoys from the Bristol Channel up the Irish Sea to Belfast Loch. From there, having gathered in more ships from Liverpool and the Clyde to form a larger convoy with more escort vessels, the task was to take the convoy around the north of Ireland into the Atlantic until out of the range of enemy aircraft. HMS *Pozarica* would then rendezvous with an incoming convoy and escort it in to Belfast Loch and (in part) onwards to the Bristol Channel. This particular task was known to the crew as the "Milk Run". I stayed with the ship, sleeping in the sick bay, until we reached Belfast Loch, where I was put ashore at Bangor to await the return trip. I was back in Milford Haven in less than two weeks. On the way north to Belfast Loch we had sailed in darkness and had opened up with all the ship's high angle 4" guns at German bombers over-flying the convoy on their way to bomb Liverpool or Manchester. This was a deafening experience for me. I was allowed to stand at the back of the bridge when the ship went to action stations and I was very impressed by the power and noise of a "Shoot" of all the ship's heavier guns. I have no idea whether we did any damage to the enemy aircraft but we must have surprised and shaken them, for we were in the middle of the Irish Sea and they would not have been expecting AA fire from there. The return journey to Milford Haven was without incident and, when I bade farewell and good luck to my father, neither of us realized then that we would not be seeing one another again until after the war, nearly five years later. While with him I had told my father that, having failed at the second attempt to get into the Royal Navy as a Paymaster Cadet, I now intended to enlist in the Army. He hid his disappointment and was understanding and supportive, giving me every encourage-ment. In June/July 1942 HMS *Pozarica* was part of the close escort for the ill-fated North Russia "scatter" convoy PQ17, but she managed to reach Archangel unscathed, with little ammunition left, after a voyage of almost continuous action against enemy aircraft and submarines. She brought six surviv-ing merchant ships in with her, each heavily laden with war equipment for the Russians. In early 1943, at about the time when I was marching into Burma for the first time, HMS *Pozarica* was attacked by fifteen enemy torpedo bombers while escorting a supply convoy into the port of Bône in North Africa and, although beached, became a total loss. The aft gun deck and "Y" turret were a shambles and there were over forty casualties but, by the grace of God, the rest of the crew of 300, including my father, survived to fight another day.

All this activity "in aid of the war effort" by members of my family and many of my friends made me more determined than ever to get off my backside and do something myself. Soon after my sister's return to England from South America I left our home in Hampstead and a short time later found myself being enlisted as a volunteer private soldier in the Royal Scots. I did not have to present myself for medical examination and the final formalities of enlistment until the following day, so I returned home and my mother listened with a certain amount of resignation while I told her that I had joined up in the Army. She slowly got used to the idea and, because my father was at sea aboard HMS *Pozarica*, I gave him the news by letter. Induction, kitting out and the seemingly non-stop activity of recruit training followed. This was very much simpler for me than for most of the other recruits because of my enthusiastic participation in the activities of the OTC at my school during the previous few years. Foot drill, rifle drill and weapon training presented no problems and, with this somewhat unfair advantage, it was inevitable that I stood out somewhat among the other recruits. I also had "Cert A" from the OTC and so I suppose it was not surprising that I was called forward for interview as a potential officer when the six weeks of primary training came to an end. The interview with an exalted personage holding the rank of Brigadier was a bit of a farce. War Office Selection Boards (WOSBs) had not yet been introduced. I remember I was asked:

1. What my father did; answer: regular officer in the Royal Navy (good, good!)
2. Where I went to school; answer: UCS (good, good!)
3. What games I played; answer: rugby football (ah! very good!)

It seemed that my "Cert A" and a satisfied interviewing Brigadier gave me a passport to becoming an Officer Cadet. I did not complain. I awaited the result of my interview with the hope that things would turn out well, and so it was. 3066386 Private R.P.D.F. Painter was ordered to proceed to Ramillies Barracks, Aldershot, for "officer training at an OCTU to be designated". This then was my very first step on the ladder of an Army career.

Chapter 2

TOWARDS THE EAST

So it had come to this. I was to leave this famous infantry regiment, the First of Foot. The Royal Scots are the right of the line and oldest established regular infantry regiment in the British Army; for this reason they are affectionately known as "Pontius Pilate's Bodyguard". I was leaving almost as soon as I had joined as a volunteer, for I had just completed my basic training as an infantryman and was now an officer cadet in Ramillies Barracks, Aldershot. It was a very cold winter and at the beginning of December 1941 I was expecting to go to an OCTU in the United Kingdom; and now, within the space of a few days, all that had changed and I was drawing tropical kit from the QM Stores while the snow pelted down outside. Half of my draft had been informed that we were to do our officer training in India and would be leaving shortly for the Far East.

During the first two weeks of December 1941 I was still clad in my battle dress, topped by a tam o'shanter. The only difference was that I was no longer with the training battalion of the Royal Scots, but was a member of a draft of officer cadets awaiting shipment to India. The uniform of a private soldier in the Royal Scots, which I had been wearing for the last few months, was just the same as before, except that it now sported a white strip around the headband of my tam o'shanter and white flashes on each shoulder to inform the world that I had now become one of the lowest forms of animal life in the Army, the unfortunate officer cadet. We soon found that we were resented by private soldiers, pitied and treated with extreme caution by older soldiers and NCOs and regarded with suspicion and a certain amount of contempt by junior officers. Perhaps the latter felt that they had "made it" and we hadn't a hope of doing so!

When our departure became more definite, preparations increased apace and I remember very clearly visiting the Cambridge Hospital in Aldershot for various essential inoculations and vaccinations. I think we had to make at least three visits to the hospital and each one was through thick snow in the late afternoon, when darkness had fallen and it was bitterly cold. One or two of the inoculations were quite unpleasant to the uninitiated and I recall that most of us were cheerful going to the hospital but somewhat sorry for ourselves as we took the long walk back to Ramillies Barracks, nursing aching arms and imagining that a fever was developing. At last preparations were completed, we said our goodbyes to our girlfriends in the town, packed our kitbags and watched for our final orders to begin the long journey ahead of us. When it happened, it happened fast. We were in our barrack rooms in Ramillies Barracks at about six in the evening and we were told by the subaltern who was to be our conducting officer on the journey to get outside with our kit and climb into the back of one of the 3-ton lorries waiting there. By seven o'clock that evening we were sitting squashed in compartments of a troop train in a siding near Aldershot Station. Blackout was normal at that time as a general "Air Raid Precaution" throughout Britain and there were no lights in the station, on the train or in the streets of the town. We sat in complete darkness in the troop train as it rumbled northwards throughout the night. I remember the only stop was at Carlisle at about 5 in the morning. By this time influenza, which had been developing, had really overtaken me and I was feeling quite ill. Perhaps the inoculations had made matters worse. I remember staggering on to the station platform, having dragged my mess tin from my pack with the object of joining a queue for some tea. When I reached the tea urn, I held out the mess tin to be filled; I noticed the tea was very frothy but went quickly back to my seat in the train to drink it. A packet of washing powder must have split in my pack, for the tea tasted of hot soap. This then was my breakfast before embarkation. We moved on and eventually stopped at Greenock, alongside

14

the quay, where an enormous ship awaited us. This was the SS *Stratheden*, an old P&O liner which had been converted for troopship duties. By the time I had staggered up the gangway and was on board the ship, I felt very feverish and must have looked so ill that I was taken off to the ship's sickbay. There I was consigned to a cot, in which I remained for the first week of the voyage. This was very comfortable and I thought myself most fortunate, but when I eventually rejoined the rest of my draft in G5 port mess deck, I found that a goodly proportion of my kit had disappeared – no doubt scrounged or pinched by those who were short of the items concerned. The mess deck was extremely crowded and I found that we slept either in hammocks, on mess tables or on the floor. In fact, the SS *Stratheden* was carrying 4,500 male soldiers and some 500 female nursing staff, all bound for India, although the ship was originally designed to carry less than 1,000 passengers.

The ship had sailed while I was in the sickbay and, by the time I had the opportunity of seeing the outside world again, we must have been well out into the North Atlantic. When I went up on deck for the first time since embarkation, I saw that we were part of an enormous convoy moving in four lanes and with a number of escort vessels busily protecting our flanks.

The convoy turned from a westerly course to a southerly course at about this time and for many days we steamed slowly southwards and the weather became warmer. Soon we were able to take turns at sleeping on deck to relieve the congestion below. In due course we arrived at the bay of Freetown in Sierra Leone and here we stayed at anchor for a week, although none of us was allowed ashore. The troopships were constantly surrounded by dug-out canoes with naked natives diving for coins and offering fruit for sale to the soldiers hanging over the rail. A number of them insisted on giving explicit displays of various portions of their anatomy to the watching soldiers, much to the dismay (or was it delight?) of the small female contingent on board the *Stratheden*. Anyway, someone must have complained, for the ship's high pressure hoses were directed towards these miscreants with such effect that they gave up their vulgarities and made off towards other troopships of the convoy anchored in the bay. The stay at Freetown was very tedious because of the sultry heat, unrelieved by the breezes that normally kept the ship cool when we were under way at sea. During this week we spent much of our time sleeping, trying to keep clean and playing housey-housey in illegal schools organized by the more criminal elements amongst the soldiers on board. We were rarely called upon to do any military duties and, although the shore looked luscious and inviting, the stay at Freetown was without doubt the most unpleasant week of this long voyage.

Eventually the day came when we weighed anchor and the convoy reformed off the coast of Sierra Leone for the journey southwards towards the Cape.

As we formed again into four columns, we noticed that the escort had been considerably reduced and assumed that, because of the increased ranges, the danger of attack by submarine had now passed. The convoy took a south-westerly course so that we travelled in the mid-Atlantic for much of the journey to the Cape of Good Hope, turning on to an easterly course when we were level with Cape Town. After we left Freetown we began to see the wonders of the sea in the tropics. The appearance of flying fish became a daily occurrence, we were followed for days by schools of porpoise, hopeful sharks kept us company and the sunrise and sunset each day were so beautiful that even the most coarse and unimaginative among us could be deeply moved. We all preferred the opportunity of sleeping on deck to the cramped and smelly confines of the mess decks. The only disadvantage of sleeping in the open was that the Lascar seamen began washing and scrubbing down the decks at about 4 in the morning and our first warning (and often our last) before being drenched to the skin by salt water from a hose directed towards us was the cry "water coming, water coming".

Throughout the voyage the officer cadets of my draft, who were bound for officer training with the ultimate aim of commissioning into the Indian Army, were given daily instruction in elementary Urdu by a Major of the regular Indian Army, who happened to be travelling on board to rejoin his regiment. He was in effect a British equivalent of the "munshi" or Indian language instructor we were to meet throughout our officer cadet training once we had settled in Bangalore. We had language classes for about an hour each day throughout the voyage in the *Stratheden* and, by the time we arrived in Bombay, we were beginning to speak some colloquial Urdu. Facility in the language was essential if we were to be able to communicate with the Indian soldiers who eventually would come under our command.

Apart from this, there was very little to occupy us during the long days of this part of the voyage. We always seemed to be hungry and, after casting our eyes on the food being carried in by waiters to the officers' dining saloon, we learnt to supplement our rations by hanging about at the exit through which the waiters passed, so that we could remove some of the tasty pieces that had been left over by the diners, but which were still very palatable compared with the uninteresting rations on which we were expected to live. During this period, although I was about to start training to be an officer, my opinion of officers was at a fairly low ebb. This did not improve for any of us as we watched with envious eyes the activities of these exalted persons with nursing sisters on the sun deck of the ship at night.

Because of the zig-zag of normal convoy movement and the wide diversion into the middle of the South Atlantic to travel from Sierra Leone to the Cape, this part of the journey took more than three weeks and we were delighted when at last we sighted land and realized that we would have a spell ashore again. The convoy divided into two parts, one of which went to Cape Town and the other, including the *Stratheden*, went to Durban. In preparation for going ashore in South Africa, we were all subjected to somewhat pompous lectures about the dangers of drinking Cape brandy (apparently a very potent brew) and the care we should take about open discussion concerning the colour bar and dire warnings of the consequence of mixing with half-castes, particularly females. Needless to say, all these warnings tended to stimulate many private soldiers to do exactly what they had been told not to do as soon as they set foot on shore. As we sailed into the harbour at Durban we were greeted by an enormously fat woman who stood at the end of the Mole at the harbour entrance singing popular and patriotic songs with an operatic voice, aided by a loud hailer.

Stratheden made fast to the quayside and we looked eagerly at this new and strange land. We noticed a very large number of civilian cars parked nearby and it soon became apparent that these belonged to white South Africans who had come to invite British soldiers to their homes and entertain them while we stayed for a few days in their country. The word soon spread around the ship that this was the case and there was much eagerness to obtain permission to go ashore. I was sent for by the ship's RSM almost as soon as we arrived and was informed that I would be required for a 24-hour spell of gangway sentry duty on this first day in Durban. Unfortunately for me this put paid to the chances of becoming the guest of one of the families in the waiting cars alongside the ship, for there were many more soldiers than invitations. I found myself standing at the bottom of one of the gangways, with rifle and fixed bayonet, and so remained off and on for the next 24 hours. Eventually I escaped from the ship and had a chance of seeing Durban. The beaches were beautiful, with sweeping bays and a large expanse of sand. We had been warned of sharks but the bathing was superlative. Near one of the best beaches I visited a snake farm, which was evidently one of the sights of the town, and I was fascinated by the wide variety of reptiles and snakes to be seen there.

The town itself had wide streets and a pleasant atmosphere. We were all impressed by the hospitality of the white population and depressed by the subjugation of the blacks who all appeared to accept a servile existence. This was particularly surprising because the majority of the black population of Durban was Zulu and these were perhaps the most dignified and physically well constructed of the native population, with a long history of warrior-type existence. It was depressing to see these fine men between the shafts of rickshaws, although I must confess that I had a ride myself and sat in a pungent atmosphere of Zulu sweat as I was pulled up and down the main street of the town. The local white population were no doubt most upset by the sight late one evening of drunken Australian soldiers between the shafts of rickshaws, running races up and down the road with Zulus as passengers in the vehicles. I tried the Cape brandy against the advice of my betters and found that it wasn't too bad, but I think I avoided discussing the colour bar and so did not get myself involved in any heated arguments on the subject. Each

18

evening we returned to the ship and, provided we were free from military duties, we returned the following day to the town to continue our exploration of the wonders of Durban. These seemed to have exhausted themselves after five or six days and I was not sad to be told that we were leaving to continue our journey on the seventh day after our arrival. One officer cadet from my draft had disappeared while we were in Durban. The story was that he had won a large amount of money on a horse on the first day there and had not been seen since. We heard no more of him and he certainly did not rejoin us in Bangalore.

When all, except our missing colleague, had re-embarked on *Stratheden*, we sailed from Durban and the same fat lady was on the Mole singing to see us on our way. The convoy reformed, but we noticed that the formation had changed and it was really two convoys in one. We steamed north-eastwards up the African coast with a light escort, passing through the channel between Madagascar and the mainland. For much of the time we were in sight of the island to the east of us.

As we cleared the northern tip of Madagascar we watched half the convoy disappear towards the east and Singapore. We were later to learn that they arrived on the day of the surrender to the Japanese and everyone in that half of the convoy became prisoners of war as soon as they set foot in the Far East. Our half of the convoy was still an impressively large number of ships and we, the more fortunate ones, continued our journey northwards towards Bombay. We arrived off the western coast of India before dawn on 3 February 1942. By good fortune it was my turn to be sleeping on deck as we made landfall and steamed into Bombay and I have a vivid recollection of the sun rising over the coast and my first sight of the mainland of India from the deck of the ship. As we moved up the estuary and it became lighter, we could see the dhows and fishing vessels and smell the distinctive smells of the bazaar for the first time. Eventually SS *Stratheden* tied up at Ballard Pier, Bombay, and we began to disembark. Because of the numbers involved, disembarkation took many hours, but eventually our draft was hurried on to a collection of third class rail carriages, which were to become our home for the next three days. Each compartment was equipped with seats similar to the wooden slatted park benches one finds in England. There were no comforts and sleeping arrangements were what could be made of these surroundings. At about 10 o'clock that night the train eventually pulled out of Bombay and we began our long journey to Bangalore. This uncomfortable trip by railway, with no washing or sleeping facilities and the bare necessities of food and drink, lasted three days and three nights. By the time we reached the outskirts of Bangalore we were very scruffy soldiers, although we had done the best we could to maintain some sort of standards. The heat during the journey had been extreme for the uninitiated and, having only just landed in India, we were of course completely un-acclimatized. As a consequence, although we were all young and fit, it was hardly an enjoyable journey.

The arrival in Bangalore was such a complete and startling contrast to the conditions that we had met both in the troop-ship and on the three-day journey by rail that we found the new order difficult to accept or believe. We were met at Bangalore rail station by representatives of the Officer Training School (OTS) and were swiftly transported to the OTS just outside the town. On arrival, we were overwhelmed by the efficiency of the staff who were there to receive us and settle us in. In no time at all we had each been allocated a room, a personal servant, two complete changes of uniform clothes which seemed to fit and, within an hour and a half of setting foot in the OTS, we were all bathed, shaved, properly clothed and sitting down to an enormous and sumptuous meal in the OTS Cadets' Mess. To our amazement everyone was extremely polite to us and we were treated like human beings for the first time in many months. The more cynical among us felt there had to be a catch somewhere and, of course, there was. On the following day we began our officer training in earnest and, for the next six months, our feet touched the ground only on rare occasions; but throughout this period it would be fair to say that the staff treated us as though we were already commissioned, a situation which was quite the opposite to that applying at the time in OCTUs in England.

My memories of the OTS are of energetic basic infantry train-ing and also prolonged periods of close-quarter and unarmed combat training, under the tender care of a ferocious but understanding APTC warrant officer; of enormous meals in the Mess to the accompaniment of Indian music from All India Radio; of ending each day, particularly in the first three months, in a state of complete exhaustion and of welcoming sleep. I was amazed to find, having just come from a war-torn Britain where people were working and fighting for their lives and where the sharp cutting edge of snobbery and class-consciousness was being blunted by the prevailing conditions, that the curriculum at the OTS included items which were truly Victorian in nature. We were taught the correct procedures for "dropping cards" and signing the visitors' book on arrival at a new station in India. The etiquette of introducing oneself to the social life of a cantonment seemed to be of great importance and this was at a time when the battles with the advancing Japanese in the first Burma campaign were raging and our forces were being thoroughly trounced in their first encounters with a brutal enemy. To be fair, much of our training was relevant and the basic Junior Leader field and weapon training and tactics for infantry officers were excellent. However, there was a general air of unreality about the place, of attitudes which were more appropriate to the turn of the century than to the requirements for fighting a war of survival. We took it all in good heart, for frankly we enjoyed the feeling that we were being taught to be "Sahibs" in the old style, but in the back of our minds there remained the feeling that the cold realities of war would over-take us swiftly as soon as we tasted action against the Japanese for the first time. I was to meet this air of unreality again as soon as I was granted my emergency commission from the OCTU at Mhow some months later. My first railway warrant as a 2nd Lieutenant, to cover my journey from Mhow to Meerut, included a horse box which was attached to the rear of the train to accommodate my charger. I did not possess a horse for my personal use and was unlikely ever to do so, but the horse box was provided as a matter of course. We were also warned con-stantly that it was socially unacceptable for officers to associate with Anglo-Indian ladies at any time. Fortunately most of these irrelevant codes of behaviour and wasteful items of training were dropped as the war progressed, particularly after the arrival of Mountbatten as Supreme Commander, but at the time they did no good and some undoubted harm to our preparation for war.

During the last three months of our training our time was spent on infantry exercises, during the course of which each of us in turn took periods of command. These exercises involved travelling through the surrounding countryside and, although this stage of our training was stimulating and very tiring, the exercises also gave us an opportunity of meeting the local village people and of seeing a bit more of India than just the inside of the OTS. It was during this period that we had our first opportunity to make use of free time in the evenings. With a certain amount of timidity we explored the bazaars and the very limited nightlife of Bangalore. The more brave among us crept into the "European Only" Club and crept out again very quickly, as we were obviously not welcome and would not be so until commissioned. We found places to drink and sometimes had too much. I remember on one occasion after an evening in Bangalore a collection of us were returning to the OTS on bicycles after a good night out. Remarkably these bicycles were provided by the Army, which even went to the extent of developing a highly complicated drill so that we could move on bicycles in organized parties; such commands as "prepare to mount" followed by "mount" were often followed by a disastrous collision and a pile of twisted bicycles and bruised cadets. On this occasion I had had far too much to drink and did not, at that stage in my life, know how to cope with this. I was leading the "pack" on my bicycle and completely missed a left hand turn in the road. Riding straight on, I went up a bank, down the other side and into 6 feet of green water, still astride my bike. When I emerged – I am told I was roaring with laughter – I remember noticing a whole crowd of my companions lined up on the top of the bank roaring with laughter at me. Eventually I was hauled back on to the road by my friends and we all rode home to the OTS.

At some time during the last two months of my training at Bangalore the permanent staff asked me to help them with the training of cadets in the use of morse code. Apparently it was a rule at that time that no cadet could be commissioned until he had passed a test of ten words per minute morse. Although the School was extremely well equipped, it appeared that there was nobody on the staff who knew the morse code. They had noted from my records that I was an amateur morse operator and I was asked to help. As a consequence I found myself from time to time sitting in front of an assembly of fellow cadets, tapping away at the key of a morse buzzer while they tried to keep up and transcribe what I was sending. One day the OTS was visited by a Colonel from Royal Signals, who was obviously scavenging around infantry training units to find possible officer material for Royal Signals in India. I noticed this officer standing at the back of the class when I was doing my act with the buzzer. Later I was summoned to the Commandant's office and introduced to the visiting Royal Signals officer. I was then given a prolonged pep talk which, in summary, said that I was wasting my time in the infantry; that I should transfer to the Signals Training Centre (STC) at Mhow immediately. Would I volunteer to do so? He then proceeded to extol the virtues of Royal Signals and I was so impressed that I agreed. As a result of all this I left my comrades at the OTS at Bangalore a month before they were commissioned into Indian infantry regiments and moved to Mhow to join No 20 Course at the Royal Signals OCTU for a further four months' training as a cadet.

At that time the OCTU at Mhow was commanded by "Dinty" Moore, a somewhat eccentric Lieutenant Colonel, and the Senior Warrant Officer was the famed RSM Garoni, the same Garoni who had three teenaged daughters said to be kept constantly under lock and key for fear of unwelcome approaches by the soldiery.

No 20 Course was the largest that had been mustered at the Mhow OCTU up to that time. Most of the cadets had just arrived from the United Kingdom and so, in one sense, I was considered to be a veteran although I was still only 19 years old, having been in India for the previous six months as an infantry cadet. On the other hand, most of the other cadets of 20 Course were much older than I, some being really ancient (to my young mind) at 30, even 35 years old. As in my case, all had been selected as potential officers from service in the ranks of the wartime Army and had been sent to India for their Royal Signals OCTU course. I was the only cadet on the course who had already completed most of an infantry OCTU training. As a consequence some of the syllabus was repetitious for me, particularly in the earlier part of the course; but it was well worth doing again and my "double dose" certainly helped me to achieve a good final grading and was most useful in the days to come when we were fighting the war in earnest. We were taught signals tactics and introduced to the subtleties of wireless and field cable communications. We were given regular flag drill (single flag visual signalling using the morse code) and worked with heliographs and "Lamps, daylight, signalling". Our introduction to the wonders of the telephone exchange was restricted mainly to the "10 line UC" and field telephones, but, as my entire service as a junior officer during the remainder of the war was with brigade signal sections, this was most appropriate. We were taught how to erect and maintain poled open wire PL routes. Some of our number were doomed to spend many months of the next few years building a PL route from India into Persia to no real purpose. We learned all there was to know about motorcycle, jeep and horse "despatch rider services". The depth of our purely technical training into the signalling equipment of the day would be considered entirely inadequate in modern times but it sufficed and we had a thorough training in equipment operation, maintenance and handling. We were also introduced to mule transport, a boon as far as I was concerned, as I was seldom without mules in Burma once I had been sent up to the fighting. Signal priorities and security classifications were all drummed into us and we were given a basic introduction into the ciphers and codes of the day. Above all, we exercised and exercised until we longed to be free of it all and to be given an opportunity of practising the arts of field communications in real rather than training surroundings.

Our Officer Commanding "Officer Training Company" was Major David Horsfield, a young regular officer who ran the officer training with startling efficiency, understanding and, when necessary, with an iron hand. Unbeknown to me – he never mentioned it – he had come through the whole 1942 retreat from Burma and was already experienced in the unpleasant ways of the Japanese soldier.

I found the course to be excellent, informative and an education in itself. We had to work very hard and there was no sympathy for shirkers, the worst of whom were sent back to their units (RTU'd) as private soldiers. The rest of us struggled on and took our "Punishment Parades" at 3 a.m. – a drill session for an hour in darkness as penance for our sins – with resignation and a sneaking realization that we probably deserved a much worse fate. Eventually the great day dawned and those of us who had survived were commissioned as Second Lieutenants in the Royal Signals and awaited our postings to units. Much to my surprise I was awarded an 'A' cadet rating and was summoned to New Delhi for an interview with my shiny new pip on each shoulder. All my contemporaries had left for units by this time but I still did not know my fate.

After the train journey to New Delhi I found myself in a large comfortable office, the walls of which were covered with maps. I was greeted by a heavily built Staff Colonel who invited me to sit down, asked me how I had enjoyed my course at Mhow and congratulated me on my commissioning. He then asked me very directly how I would feel about walking from India to China across Burma, with elephants and mules as transport. At first he made the whole proposition sound like a holiday hike and then I began to realize that I was being introduced to something entirely different from the normal run of things in the Burma war. In this way I was introduced to Wingate's "Long Range Penetration Groups" (LRPG). At the end of the interview I was completely sold to the whole idea and had volunteered to join "Special Force" – the alternative name at that time for LRPG, which changed again later to the "Chindits". I was told to return to Mhow immediately, to take my ten days' commissioning leave and then to report to Meerut for further instructions. Within a few weeks of my interview in New Delhi, I was to start the long walk into enemy held Burma, as green as any young Second Lieutenant could be but eager to learn fast and obliged to do so by circumstances and experience.

When I returned to Mhow I was able to complete all the formalities and catch a train for Bombay on the same day. I travelled on the narrow gauge railway running from Indore to Khandwa Junction, where we had to change to the broad gauge railway on the main line from Delhi to Bombay. I had already arranged to meet some old family friends who had offered to

25

provide me with a bed for the ten days' leave I had been granted. The train arrived at 10 p.m. and there on the platform I saw Bill Adcock and his wife, Hilda, who took me away in their car to their lovely flat at Breech Candy. The flat was on the fourth floor and from the long veranda there was a beautiful view over the beach. They gave me a most comfortable bedroom and, after a sumptuous evening meal, I went to bed. During the next few days Bill Adcock went out of his way to show me everything of interest in Bombay and to ensure that I enjoyed this first period of leave since I had arrived in India. A series of visits for lunch to the Gymkhana Club and Greens Restaurant were interspersed with numerous parties to give me an opportunity of meeting people. Bill and Hilda Adcock could not have done more for me and I wonder sometimes whether I showed them how much I appreciated their kindness.

As I knew it must, this welcome ten-day break came to an end. I had very much enjoyed my stay with the Adcocks, not only because it was a complete rest and change but also because it helped me to become accustomed to this new experience of being a commissioned officer at last. My kind hosts took me by car to the main railway terminal in Bombay and put me on the express to New Delhi where I was to change for the connection to Meerut. I was to see them again nearly three years later when I was considering whether or not to return to Europe or to remain for a further year in India. I was very grateful to them for their kindness and was sad to leave, although I was eager to join an elite unit on active service.

I was to discover that the unit in Meerut was merely a staging post, a transit organization where I was to be kitted out and briefed for the march into Burma. My instructions had been to join 111 Brigade Signal Section but I found that the Brigade had not yet been formed and in due course I was cross-posted to 77 Brigade, a formation of LRPG which had been training for months in the Central Provinces. The Brigadier was Orde Wingate and the Brigade was about to set off into Burma on his first expedition. I finally caught up with them in mid-February 1943 near Imphal, where they were taking a short rest after marching from railhead at Dimapur and before setting off again for Tamu and the River Chindwin. I had been flown in by

Dakota to Tulihal airstrip from Calcutta's Dum Dum Airport, a raw Second Lieutenant who had missed the specialist training in the Central Provinces and who, in retrospect, was far too young and inexperienced to participate in such a venture. But there I was, 19 years old, fit and overflowing with enthusiasm. I was soon to learn the hard way that what lay ahead was far from being a picnic.

Chapter 3

FIRST WINGATE
LONG RANGE PENETRATION 1943
A RAID CALLED OPERATION "LONGCLOTH".

I was not expected. Nobody seemed to know that I was coming to join the Brigade and there was little or no interest in my arrival. I felt like the proverbial fish out of water. By this time all operational elements of the Brigade were down in the Kabaw Valley near Tamu and only rear elements remained on the Imphal plain. A base staff officer (I think he was a DAA & QMG) finally examined the Movement Order I had been given at Meerut and I was told, "I suppose you had better join Colonel Alexander with No 1 Group". This meant very little to me until it was explained to me that the Brigade Signal Officer, whose name was Spurlock, would already have left Tamu with the Brigadier and the "Northern" Group (which turned out to be the bulk of the Brigade as it included Nos 3, 4, 5, 7 and 8 Columns as well as the Brigade Headquarters element with Wingate).

A truck was arranged to take me down to Tamu and thence south-eastwards to catch up with the "Southern" Group, commanded by Lieutenant Colonel L.A. Alexander of 3/2 Gurkha Rifles (GR) and which was composed of No 1 Column (Major George Dunlop MC, Royal Scots) and No 2 Column (Major Arthur Emmett, 3/2 GR). Both these were Gurkha Columns. I caught up with them on the march after a hectic drive over the hills from Imphal and into the Kabaw Valley. I sought out and reported to Colonel Alexander, a Scot with a pleasant

28

but businesslike manner who soon won my respect. The truck went back up the track in a cloud of dust to return to Imphal and I began the long march into Burma.

In the next few days and nights I learnt a lot about the composition of 77 Brigade and began to understand something of our plans and intentions. In fact, we were not yet an "elite unit". Up to now, 77 Brigade had not been in action as a composite formation. We had yet to earn our laurels and live up to the title "Special Force" which would be given to us. The Brigade was made up of a British infantry battalion, the 13th King's Liverpool, a battalion of Gurkhas, the 3/2 Gurkha Rifles, and the 2nd Battalion Burma Rifles. To these were added 142 Commando Company (a unit derived from Calvert's "Bush Warfare School", formed in Maymyo in early 1942) and a variety of specialists who included not only Royal Engineers, Royal Signals and RAF Personnel but also animal transport specialists and some with expert personal knowledge of the country through which we would pass.

The British battalion had been on coastal defence in England earlier in the war and had been moved to India as garrison troops. Before training in the jungles of the Central Provinces, it had been considered to be a second-rate battalion but, after much weeding out (which included replacement of the Commanding Officer) and intense jungle warfare training in the style of Wingate, I was told that it was now a very much improved fighting unit, although of reduced strength because of the ruthless process of weeding out. I suspected that had I joined the Brigade earlier, during the training period in the CP, I myself might have been weeded out, merely on grounds of youthfulness and lack of experience, if for no other reason. I had only joined at the last moment and "straight from the egg" because some staff officer had thought it to be a good idea and because 111 Brigade, the second Brigade of "Special Force", had not yet been formed at that time, although I had been posted to it.

3/2 Gurkha Rifles was a wartime-raised battalion lacking in officers who could speak fluent Gurkhali or who had active service experience. The battalion had not yet been in action, although it had done well in a period of intense jungle warfare

29

training.

The Burma Rifles battalion, commanded by Lieutenant Colonel L.G. Wheeler, a much respected officer who was revered both by his soldiers and by the Kachins and Karens, was first class, loyal and invaluable in the jungles of their home country. Their intelligence-gathering techniques, contacts with the local population and other activities would make an enormous contribution to our survival in the coming months. The battalion was split up so that strong elements of Burma Rifles (BURRIFS) were part of every Column, forming Reconnaissance Platoons.

The Brigade was divided into seven Columns. I learnt that it had been the original intention to have eight Columns – four British and four Gurkha – but so many of the King's Liverpool had been sacked as unsuitable during the months of training (quite a few left for medical reasons) that there were now only three British Columns (Nos 5, 7 and 8) and four Gurkha Columns (Nos 1, 2, 3 and 4). In time I learnt also that our Brigadier, Orde Wingate, had no time for soldiers of the Indian Army and was even a little doubtful about the fighting qualities of the Gurkhas. On both counts his judgment in this respect was seriously flawed, for the best of the Indian Army proved themselves to be among the best in the world and the Gurkhas, when properly led, were invariably as brave as lions; without either, the war against the Japanese in Burma could certainly not have been won.

Each Column, commanded by a Major, was composed of approximately 400 men, fifteen horses and over 100 mules. The backbone of the Column was an enlarged company of infantry, carrying normal infantry weapons. Vickers medium machine guns, carried on mules until brought into action, gave added firepower to the Column Support Platoon and most officers carried a Thompson sub-machine gun as personal weapon in addition to a .38 revolver. (At Meerut I had been issued with a Thompson sub-machine gun – a "Tommy gun". I was to carry this heavy, clumsy weapon throughout my march on "LONGCLOTH" and learned to detest it.)

Each Column had a Commando Platoon which included a Royal Engineer element for such activities as demolitions, booby traps, sabotage and river crossings. There were Royal Signals detachments, equipped with Australian-manufactured FS6 sets, for wireless communications from each Column back to base in India and to Brigade Headquarters in the field. Unfortunately the signal plan – in my opinion, not a good one – required us to send and receive all signals for other Columns through Brigade Headquarters, with the resultant inevitable pile-up of traffic. We did not hold ciphers for use between us and other Columns and could therefore only contact them direct and "in clear" in cases of dire emergency, because of the risk of possible interception by the enemy. Within each Column there were a small number of "21" sets for short range communications "in clear" with patrols and detachments. There was also a Royal Air Force (RAF) section and wireless detachment, for selection of suitable supply dropping zones (DZ's) and for signalling to base our requests for supply drops, giving details of locations and requirements. The wireless equipment used by these RAF detachments was the "1086" set – HF high power and extremely cumbersome and heavy. It had to be broken down into three or four mule loads and took some time to unload, assemble and get on the air. I was told that the RAF officers in command of these RAF sections (they were mostly Flight Lieutenants) had volunteered for Special Duties in the belief that these would be hazardous *flying* duties. They had been horrified to find they had let themselves in for a session of marching over hundreds of miles through the jungle. However, they stuck with it and most proved to be first class in this "infantry" role.

Colonel Alex received me with courtesy but some surprise, for he was not expecting a young Second Lieutenant from Royal Signals to join him as a reinforcement, especially at this late stage and without the benefit of the months of hard training all the others had been through. As we marched along he questioned me about my background and, when I told him that I had all but completed an infantry OCTU course before my Royal Signals OCTU, he told me that he would be glad to have me provided I made myself useful, that it was now too late to send me back anyway and that the experiences of the weeks to come would no doubt do me a lot of good. Thus I was accepted as an "extra file" and began to settle in to the routine and to learn a great deal as we progressed.

The Northern Group, which was the bulk of the Brigade and included the Brigadier, his Brigade Major and the Brigade Signal Officer, had marched out of their staging area near Tamu in a north-easterly direction before I arrived. As a consequence, I did not meet them. They continued to march at night, as had been the case all the way from railhead at Dimapur, and rested up during daylight hours. Marching in darkness from Dimapur to Imphal, and onwards from Imphal to Tamu, had been partly for security but mainly to avoid the many convoys of military vehicles using the road to the supply depots on the Imphal plain and also to the Moreh Depot near Tamu. For their approach march along jungle tracks to the River Chindwin and the chosen crossing point at Tonhe, the march for them was still in darkness but now this was purely for security reasons, to minimize the possibility that the Japanese would learn of their movement into Burma. Colonel Alex explained to me that our task in the Southern Group during the earlier stages of the raid was to mislead and confuse the Japanese, and thus cover the crossing of the main body of the Brigade to the north of us, by making sure they knew of our presence when we had crossed the Chindwin to the south of Sittaung. We would then "disappear" into the jungle and head eastwards, to rejoin the rest of the Brigade later in the area of the River Irrawaddy. With this plan in mind, we marched most of the way to our chosen crossing area by day, and without too much effort to conceal ourselves. Using the Tamu to Sittaung track for some of the way, we had less distance to cover than the Northern Group to reach our crossing point and so were over the river before them. I could not help feeling that we were putting our heads on the chopping block by participating in this deception plan, but, in the event, everything went smoothly. We crossed without seeing any Japanese although news of our activities must have reached the enemy soon after we disappeared towards the east.

We crossed the Chindwin on the night of 14th and throughout 15 February 1943. The crossing point was near Auktaung, a riverside village some way to the south of Sittaung. I was fascinated to watch the way the crossing was accomplished. It was evident that the drill had been practised over and over again during training, as the whole exercise was carried out in a slick and efficient manner. At first sight, the task before us seemed to me to be well nigh impossible. The river was fairly fast running and about 500 yards wide. All we had to help us were about sixteen inflatable dinghies with paddles (the largest of which could carry a maximum of six men with their personal weapons and packs, which weighed approximately 50 pounds), sufficient strong manila rope to reach across the river and back more than twice, and whatever local boats or rafts we could lay our hands on to supplement these meagre resources. The sappers also had several block and tackle pulleys. All this seemed to be entirely inadequate for a crossing by more than 800 men, in excess of 200 mules and horses and all our weapons and equipment. It seemed to me, in my ignorance, that it was going to take us a week or two to get across and that the Japanese were bound to intervene. I should not have worried.

The first across were the Burma Rifles, who paddled over in some of our inflatables. These were then brought back to the west bank. This was well in advance of the arrival of the rest of us. The main body of each Column was held back, under cover of the jungle, while preparations for the crossing were under way. The Burma Rifles reconnoitred the east bank of the river north and south of our intended landing area and also inland towards the east. The nearest Japanese in strength appeared to be some twenty miles away, although enemy patrols were known to move along the east bank from time to time. The next stage was to establish sufficient men around the landing point on the east bank to form a bridgehead perimeter. The sappers crossed in inflatables with the Commando Platoon from each Column, taking with them one end of the manila rope and two pulleys. Both of these pulleys were attached firmly to stout trees on the far bank and the rope's end was threaded through and brought back to the west bank with the returning inflatables. The ropes were pulled taut by looping through two separate pulleys attached to trees near the west bank. They were then made fast. A specialist "traveller" pulley was mounted on each tightened rope, with ropes of lighter girth attached to either side of it, one to pull it over to the other side of the river and the other (having been paid out) to pull it back again. The design of this "traveller" pulley ensured that it could not slip off or foul the main manila rope, once mounted on it. Hanging from the "traveller" were two "tether" ropes of stout cord which could be used either to secure loads or to be held by occupants of the inflatables. Thus two separate rigs, which the sappers called "power ropes", were established from one bank to the other and the crossing started in earnest. The mules and horses swam over alongside the boats and most seemed to go quite willingly. A reasonably flat beach and exit into the jungle had been selected at both locations on the far bank. Small elements from each Column were called forward at regular intervals, from the concealment of the jungle, to cross in the boats with the help of the "power ropes" and we were all over to the east side of the river in two days. The last to cross were the rear guards of each Column and finally the small detachments of sappers manning the west bank side of the "power rope" rigs. The latter recovered and brought with them all equipment used for the crossing, paddling over in inflatables. There had been few mishaps and the whole crossing was accomplished with remarkable efficiency by both Columns.

Once over, we did not hang about. No 2 Column (Emmett) moved off through the jungle to the south-east as soon as their crossing was completed. No 1 Column (Dunlop), with Group HQ (to which I was attached) in company, left soon after them, but in a more easterly direction. Both Columns pushed on as fast as they could, by forced march, to get well clear of the crossing point before making bivouac. The jungle was fairly thick and we did not use paths at this stage but moved on compass bearings. Because of the jungle, the march was in single file – column "snake", as my more experienced companions called it – and on several occasions during this particular forced march we covered our tracks by a well-practised procedure with which I soon became familiar. The Column would halt, each man and animal would turn 90 degrees (to left or to right according to the order passed back from the head of the Column – just two words from man to man: "Halt, left" or "Halt, right") and walk a set number of paces (up to 500) into the jungle, keeping in touch with the man on either side. Every man and animal would then turn back 90 degrees to face the original direction of the line of march and the march would be resumed. With the number of men and animals involved, the movement of the Column through virgin jungle in single file inevitably left a path, however much we tried to cover our tracks. These additional "jigs", to left or right, would (we hoped) help confuse any enemy patrol which might stumble across our route after we had passed by. We were particularly careful to cover our tracks for the first mile or so after leaving the river. This first forced march into enemy territory, after leaving our crossing point, was carried out at night. Trying to move fast through the jungle, in single file and in darkness, is not to be recommended as an amusing pastime but it was clear to me that my companions had trained and trained in this. The incidence of cursing, grunting and complaining was minimal and the noise level was kept remarkably low. We could have made a noise like a herd of frantic elephants as we crashed through the bush but the Gurkha soldiers of No 1 Column set an example which I was at pains to follow.

When the decision was taken to bivouac, the Column would do the 90 degree jig again and then move into an all-round defensive position in the jungle, with Column Headquarters in the centre of a rough circle. Standing patrols would be put out and frequently an ambush would be laid on the track we had been making with our own feet before the last jig just in case we were being followed. The remainder of the Column would settle down to unload, rub down and feed the animals, to cook, to eat and then to sleep.

As soon as we arrived in a bivouac area the wireless detachments would set up shop and open up either on an agreed timed schedule or on listening watch. Wireless operators always had less rest and sleep than others in the Column, as they took turns on the set throughout all rest periods while most of the other members of the Column were sleeping. There were times when cipher operators were also involved all night enciphering and deciphering signals, often by dim light under ground sheets. Whenever it was considered acceptable to do so, battery charging "chore horses" would rumble away, the noise of these small petrol engines breaking the silence of the jungle around us.

This was the general pattern of the march each day during the coming weeks, but of course there were variations dictated by circumstances and the reactions of the Japanese to our presence in "their" territory. Our task was to avoid contact with the enemy but to ensure that he knew we were there somewhere, well to the south of the main body of the Brigade, until we reached the "railway corridor" near to Kyaikthin. There we were to do as much damage to the railway as possible before crossing the River Irrawaddy and joining up with the rest of the Brigade. There was a well-defined track from Maingnyaung, a large village to the south-east of our Chindwin crossing point opposite Auktaung, to Kyaikthin on the railway between Wuntho to the north and Kanbalu to the south (this railway was, of course, the main supply route from Mandalay to Myitkyina, used by the Japanese to sustain their two divisions in North Burma). We avoided this track, for it was well used by the Japanese, and moved through the jungle parallel to but north of it, although from time to time we revealed our presence in strength at small villages where our Burma Rifles assured us word would reach the enemy, in due course, that we had been there in exaggerated strength.

After the first bivouac following the initial crossing of the Chindwin, we resumed the march to the east. A supply drop had been arranged for both Columns at a rendezvous already selected by the Burma Rifles and Flight Lieutenant Edmunds, our RAF officer at HQ 1 Group. This was to be a daytime drop at a location a day's march from the river and both Columns were to meet again there to collect their share of the drop. It was another difficult march to reach the dropping zone on time but everything went according to plan and both Columns collected a resupply which was sufficient for five days. Once again we did not hang about but moved off as soon as we had collected all our supplies, to clear the area and get ourselves once again into the obscurity of the jungle. Dakotas dropping supplies by parachute can be seen a long way off, even in Burma. No doubt this daytime drop may have helped to deceive the enemy, but we had no wish to be there should they come to investigate.

The deception plan had been augmented, soon after we had crossed the Chindwin, by the flamboyant appearance of the senior Commando officer of the Brigade, Major John Jeffries, dressed in the full regalia of a Brigadier, in a village called Ta

Nga on the east bank and well south of our crossing point at Auktaung. This village was reported clear of Japanese by the BURRIFS at the time of his visit but it was known to be a regular stopping place for enemy patrols and to include a number of known collaborators among the inhabitants. He had with him a large patrol of men from the Commando Company and the BURRIFS and apparently gave the impression that he and his companions were the Headquarters of a Brigade moving into Burma at this point. It was a brave effort which I heard about a few days after the event, when Major Jeffries and his party joined us, their task completed. They were to stay with us until after we had crossed the River Irrawaddy. Colonel Alex felt that it would not take long for news of these activities to reach the Japanese higher command.

By 18 February we were approaching Maingnyaung from the north. The BURRIF had reported a Japanese garrison there, thought to be about 200 strong, and it was decided to lay an ambush for possible patrols from this garrison. A successful ambush by our Gurkhas cut up an enemy patrol which left six dead, but the survivors disengaged and returned to Maingnyaung, where they must have reported our location with some accuracy. Mortar fire was opened from the village and a number of our mules, with their precious loads of grain for animal fodder, bolted and were lost. No 1 Column (Dunlop) moved south to pursue and cut off the Japanese, who had withdrawn from Maingnyaung, but they ran into very thick jungle. They eventually entered the village of Ywatha, on the track leading to the south-east, where they found a stock of food but no Japs. This diversion had delayed us by three days and the Group now pushed on towards the east, moving north of the Maingnyaung – Kyaikthin track but climbing to the escarpment overlooking the valley of the River Mu.

For the next three weeks we marched steadily eastwards towards the River Irrawaddy. In more open teak jungle we marched at night but in areas of thicker jungle, particularly over the two stretches of hilly country, we marched by day. For most of the time, the going was very tough and, in addition, the mules suffered from the lack of grain (lost at Maingnyaung). Some mules also became badly galled as a result of shifting loads on

37

very steep slopes. After the first supply drop we took one more before crossing the River Mu. During the next few days we began our approach to the railway corridor, moving towards Kyaikthin from the north-west. No 2 Column was also moving towards Kyaikthin but was to the south of us.

On 3 March we reached the railway at a point close to but north of Kyaikthin and our Commando Platoon and the sappers of No 1 Column blew up and demolished a railway bridge and a stretch of the railway line as we moved over it and marched on towards Hinthaw and the river at Tagaung. Except for the action at Maingnyaung, we had encountered no Japanese up to this point and could hardly believe our good luck. Unfortunately at this time we were having trouble with both our battery chargers and wireless sets and were out of communication with base, Brigade Headquarters and all other Columns for more than a week. Eventually we found the problems and solved them but this was a particularly frustrating period for me, as I was left with a feeling of inadequacy as a Royal Signals officer because of my inability to diagnose and repair a fault swiftly at that stage in my career. I vowed to myself then that I would do something about this at the earliest possible opportunity. With the optimism of youth, it did not occur to me that I might not survive to return to India. In fact, the members of the detachment and I eventually put things right as a joint effort but it took us more than eight days (whenever we halted and could work at it) and in the meantime we were lost to the outside world. Because of this failure in communications we had to do without an intended supply drop and were getting very hungry by the time we reached the Irrawaddy at Tagaung on 8 March and began to cross the river. A small BURRIF patrol, led by Lieutenant Bruce, had entered the village ahead of us and, using threats and persuasion, had managed to assemble a collection of local river boats. During the crossing we had a remarkable piece of luck. There was no sign of the Japanese and we had a trouble-free crossing, using a large sandbank near to the east bank to help us. Quick thinking by Flight Lieutenant Edmunds brought us an unscheduled supply drop, as he heard the engines of approaching Dakotas, put out markers and received the drop onto the sandbank. We discovered later that it had not been intended for us. Some other Column must have gone short, but by this time the extent of our need was such that we did not have too much of a crisis of conscience. At least we had something to eat to keep us going.

The river seemed enormously wide but we crossed without incident and with no interference from the enemy. We found ourselves marching into an area of thick jungle as we left the Irrawaddy behind us and headed east. I think we all felt very relieved to have crossed this major water obstacle successfully and we were looking forward to rejoining the bulk of the Brigade. Our relief was accentuated by news of the disaster which had apparently overtaken our sister Column in No 1 Group. As we approached the river near Tagaung to prepare for the crossing, a party of men from No 2 Column had joined us. From them we learned that their Column had approached Kyaikthin from the west, following the single track branch railway line from Yindaik to Kyaikthin, with the apparent intention of blowing up the railway station and its engineering facilities as well as destroying the railway track. For the last few miles before reaching Kyaikthin they moved through relatively open country and must have been seen. In any event, they were ambushed by a Japanese force of considerable size. The Column was taken completely by surprise, took a considerable number of casualties and was dispersed. As always, a rendezvous had been arranged to cover such eventualities so that the Column could reassemble and sort itself out at a safer location in the jungle. These men told us they had not been able to find the others and had decided to press on to and cross the River Irrawaddy in compliance with the original plan. They were very relieved to find us and to join No 1 Column. Nothing more was heard of No 2 Column, their wireless did not "come up" again and we concluded sadly that they had been overwhelmed. (In fact I found out much later, after my return to India, that Major Emmett had led the survivors of this ambush back to the River Chindwin and safety. His wireless and ciphers were lost in the ambush, as were many of his mules with their loads, and he had concluded that his Column was no longer operational. He had therefore decided to withdraw to friendly territory with the remnants of his Column – and this he did.)

The few survivors who had managed to find us after the ambush were questioned and we were told that, during the approach march towards Kyaikthin, No 2 Column had used the actual route of the Yindaik/Kyaikthin branch railway line for much of the way. Most of this final approach march took place in darkness. A fast move was made possible by following the railway track but the normal concealment of the jungle was forfeited. In addition, there was mention of the frequent use of unshielded torches to consult maps. Sadly, it was concluded that No 2 Column had probably brought upon themselves the disaster of the ambush by failing to observe the basic principles of Chindit training in concealment in enemy-held territory. A costly lesson had been learnt. There was a side-effect to the loss of No 2 Column which resulted in an extension of the period of our wireless silence for a further week, on top of the week lost due to equipment faults. Colonel Alex was reluctant to use our wireless links for a while, in case ciphers had been compromised by the loss of wireless and cipher equipment during the ambush.

Far to the north of us, near Pinbon, disaster had also overtaken No 4 Column (Bromhead), which was part of the Northern Group. The Column was ambushed near a village called Kyaungle, while marching to rejoin No 7 Column (Gilkes), No 8 Column (Scott) and Wingate with Brigade Headquarters. The centre of No 4 Column bore the brunt of the Japanese attack, most of the mules bolted and were lost and the Column was split in half and dispersed. After Bromhead had gallantly gathered together as many as he could at the rendezvous location for the day, the Column was again attacked and dispersed and, by the time the survivors reached the arranged meeting place with Wingate, Brigade Headquarters and Nos 7 and 8 Columns had gone. Bromhead was now left without wireless, few mules and little food and ammunition. He had no alternative but to take the survivors of his Column back to the Chindwin and friendly territory.

As I understood it, we in No 1 Column and HQ No 1 Group had carried out our original orders with complete success. All we had to do now was to join the rest of the Brigade east of the Irrawaddy and receive our orders for the next phase of the operation. We were once again in good wireless contact with

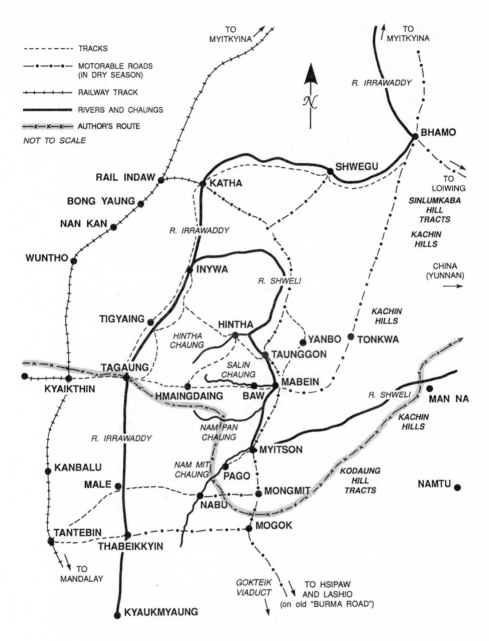

TRACKS

MOTORABLE ROADS
(IN DRY SEASON)

RAILWAY TRACK

RIVERS AND CHAUNGS

AUTHOR'S ROUTE

NOT TO SCALE

TO
MYITKYINA

TO
MYITKYINA

R. IRRAWADDY

BHAMO

SHWEGU

TO
LOIWING

SINLUMKABA
HILL
TRACTS

KACHIN
HILLS

CHINA
(YUNNAN)

RAIL INDAW

KATHA

BONG YAUNG

NAN KAN

R. IRRAWADDY

WUNTHO

INYWA

R. SHWELI

KACHIN
HILLS

TIGYAING

HINTHA

YANBO   TONKWA

HINTHA
CHAUNG

TAUNGGON

TAGAUNG

SALIN
CHAUNG

KYAIKTHIN

HMAINGDAING   BAW

MABEIN

R. SHWELI   MAN NA

KACHIN
HILLS

NAM PAN
CHAUNG

R. IRRAWADDY

MYITSON

KODAUNG
HILL
TRACTS

NAM MIT
CHAUNG   PAGO

KANBALU

MALE

MONGMIT

NAMTU

NABU

TANTEBIN

MOGOK

THABEIKKYIN

TO
MANDALAY

GOKTEIK
VIADUCT

TO HSIPAW
AND LASHIO
(on old "BURMA ROAD")

KYAUKMYAUNG

Operation "Longcloth"
February to April 1943
Sketch map of "Shweli Triangle"

41

Brigade Headquarters and our immediate problem was to move eastwards away from the river, find some secure bivouac area, preferably near water, and await further orders from Wingate. We had already marched over 250 miles through difficult country, each of us heavily laden with our framed pack and personal weapons (the "Everest" back pack weighed between 50 and 60 lbs when filled with our personal gear, emergency rations, ammunition etc). We were all somewhat worn out by now and in need of a rest in relatively safe surroundings. We were also perpetually hungry and thirsty, having been on reduced rations for some time, although the unexpected supply drop on the Irrawaddy sandbank had eased this problem for a while. I had considered myself to be extremely fit when I joined the Brigade but I was not as hard as my companions, who had been training for months in arduous conditions before coming into Burma. By this time I had lost a lot of weight, was experiencing leg ulcers (we called them jungle sores) on my shins for the first time and was beginning to feel physically a little weaker as each day went by. At least I had been acclimatized to the heat of the dry season that we were experiencing, but marching through jungle saps energy at the best of times, in spite of a daily intake of salt tablets and vitamin tablets which, in small containers, occupied a vital space in my pack. The one bright spot in our situation up to now was that I had not even seen a Japanese soldier, yet here we were, hundreds of miles inside the territory he was occupying, having blown up a stretch of his railway supply route to the north and generally having made our presence known to him. I began to realize this could not last and that, sooner rather than later, his soldiers would be buzzing around us like bees around a honey pot.

We did not know it then but our situation developed in exactly this way during the next few weeks. From discussions that I overheard and from replies to questions I put to Colonel Alex, I began to realize that we had arrived in an area which, although ideal for concealment, was not going to be easy to leave. The territory in which we now found ourselves became known as the Shweli Triangle. In fact, it was shaped more like a square box into which we had put ourselves, with the Japanese in increasing numbers covering and patrolling all sides of the square. To the west of us lay the River Irrawaddy, a water obstacle of considerable danger now that the enemy knew roughly where we were. To the north, the River Shweli ran in to the Irrawaddy at Inywa. To our east, the valley of the River Shweli, another difficult water obstacle, having changed direction with an almost ninety degree bend towards the south at a point well to the east of Inywa, ran southwards parallel to but some 40 to 50 miles from the Irrawaddy valley. At a village called Myitson, the Shweli valley turned sharply towards the east and continued in that direction into China, the river rising in the mountains of Yunnan and running from its source along this route all the way to Inywa and its confluence with the Irrawaddy. Across the southern side of the square box, there was a motorable road from the Irrawaddy towards the east, running from Thabeikkyin to Mogok (and then northwards to Mongmit). North of this road, and parallel to it, was another which ran from a village called Nabu, on the Nam Mit Chaung, to Mongmit (and then northwards to Myitson). The Nam Mit Chaung was navigable between Nabu and Myitson and was used by Japanese boat patrols, as was the River Shweli throughout the most of its length from Myitson to Inywa. There was also a good road, motorable during the dry season, from Myitson northwards. This ran eventually to Katha, with a turn-off north-eastwards to Shwegu, and it followed the course of the Shweli, and close to its east bank, for much of the way to Inywa. Thus we were "in a bag" and extricating ourselves without some severe fighting was not going to be easy.

It is all very well being wise after the event but, in retrospect, there seems little doubt that to take the entire Brigade over the Irrawaddy and into the Shweli Triangle was a grave error of judgement by Wingate.

At first we marched south-east from our landing point opposite Tagaung. The country was very heavily covered with thick jungle and soon became almost mountainous as we left the river valley. It was very hot and dry and water became a major preoccupation. Progress was very slow through this difficult terrain and there were times when a day of struggling up and down through virgin jungle was rewarded by covering a distance of only seven to ten miles. This was exhausting work and we longed for a respite.

We took another supply drop (this time it was one that was intended for us) on 14 March, by which time we were well into the hills to the south of the village of Hmaingdaing. We moved a safe distance away from the DZ and then rested up for a day. By this time we were becoming very short of water and a further move eastwards to Nam Pan Chaung became essential. On 17 March a signal from Brigade informed us that Brigade Headquarters, with No 7 Column (Gilkes) and No 8 Column (Scott), had crossed the Irrawaddy successfully at a point near to Inywa. They were now heading south-east towards the Hintha Chaung. As No 3 Column (Calvert) and No 5 Column (Fergusson) had already crossed into the Shweli Triangle, this news confirmed that the whole Brigade (less No 2 Column (Emmett) and No 4 Column (Bromhead) (survivors of both these Columns were well on their way back to India by this time) was now over the River Irrawaddy and in the Triangle.

On 18 March we received orders by wireless from Brigade to march to the area of Mogok in support of No 3 Column, which had spent the previous night in bivouac close to us. It seemed the plan was for No 3 Column and No 5 Column to march south-east to the old Burma Road and blow up the Gokteik Viaduct, which was well over 100 miles from *our* present position. We in 1 Group and No 1 Column were to follow, in support of these two Columns. We were still in desperate need of water and were obliged to continue our march eastwards to the Nam Pan Chaung, our nearest water, before turning south to comply with the order and head for the area of Mogok.

The next day we were informed by signal that No 5 Column patrols had reported a Japanese force of battalion strength at Myitson, the village where the Nam Mit Chaung joined the River Shweli. They had also reported that more Japanese in vehicles were being moved from Mongmit to Myitson to join the force already there. This was unwelcome news and seemed to indicate that the enemy were at last taking serious action in an effort to box us in and eliminate us.

On 21 March we took another large supply drop. The Japanese must have seen this air activity over us for, thanks to the efforts of our BURRIFS Reconnaissance Platoon, we just managed to evade a strong enemy patrol as we struggled onwards towards the waters of the Nam Pan Chaung. We arrived at last at a comfortable bivouac location, near to the Chaung, during the evening of 22 March. We now had plenty of water, not only to drink and use for cooking but also for washing. We had been particularly worried about our mules and they were now able to drink their fill. Next morning, 23 March, we discovered that No 5 Column was in bivouac a short distance away on the other side of the Chaung. They had not heard us arrive on the previous evening and we had not discovered their bivouac until both Columns started to use the Chaung for washing and a swim at dawn the next day. This speaks volumes not only for the density of the jungle around us but also for the extreme care taken by both Columns to keep noise, movement and lights to a minimum in our bivouac areas. We learned that new orders from Brigade had cancelled the instructions to No 5 Column to join No 3 Column and attack the Gokteik Viaduct. Instead No 5 Column was now ordered to move north and join Brigade Headquarters on the Salin Chaung near to the village of Baw. Calvert and his No 3 Column were to proceed to Gokteik as before and we were to join him for this attack. We had not yet received this change of orders from Brigade but it made little difference to us, as we were already "geared up" to march south towards Mogok.

Our chance meeting with No 5 Column was fortunate in one way, as Major Jeffries and his party left us and attached themselves to the other Column so that they could rejoin Brigade Headquarters. They had been with us since their gallant deception attempt south of Auktaung, but their correct place in the scheme of things was with Brigade. I could have accompanied them and reported myself at last to Spurlock, the Brigade Signal Officer, but it is probable that he did not even know of my existence at that time. In any event the question did not arise, as Colonel Alex had become accustomed to having me around, not only as a Royal Signals officer but often for small tasks more appropriate to the work of an infantry subaltern. He had already sent me out on small patrol jobs with BURRIFS and Gurkha soldiers on a number of occasions.

We bade farewell to No 5 Column and moved off that morning, heading south for Mogok and hoping to make contact with No 3 Column for the onward march to the Gokteik Viaduct. In bivouac that night we received an odd signal from Wingate which I will never forget. It was in clear and was a biblical reference to Genesis XIX – "Remember Lot's wife. Return not whence ye came. Seek thy salvation in the mountains". Colonel Alex and Major Dunlop puzzled over this and concluded that the signal was encouragement for us to press on to the hills beyond Mongmit, as already ordered. We had also been instructed earlier to meet a BURRIF officer (his name was Herring) at Mongmit but the date of the rendezvous had passed (Captain Herring had spent some time in the Kachin Hills south of Bhamo, trying to recruit Kachins as levies to help the Brigade). On 25 March we reached the Nam Mit Chaung between Nabu and Pago. HQ 1 Group and most of No 1 Column had crossed the Chaung when a Japanese patrol stumbled on the tail end of the Column. At the head of the line of march we heard the sounds of gunfire behind us and realized that the Column was under attack. We learned later that a sharp little fight developed but the Column rearguard, reinforced by the Platoon ahead of them which turned round to help deal with the problem, soon had the situation under control. A considerable number of casualties were inflicted on the enemy before the rearguard disengaged, withdrew into the jungle and rejoined the rest of the Column at the rendezvous point arranged for that day. We and the remainder of No 1 Column had meanwhile taken the customary evasive action to reduce the chances of the enemy following us and had marched to the same rendezvous point. This small action, in which three Gurkha riflemen were killed, had delayed us for a few hours in our march towards Mogok. It could have been much worse and by crossing the Nam Mit Chaung, which was patrolled periodically by the enemy in boats, we had put behind us one of the barriers across the south side of the "box" in which we were confined.

The next hazard to the south was the motorable track which ran between Nabu and Mongmit. We knew this was patrolled not only by enemy soldiers on foot but also by vehicles from time to time. After that we could either cross the Thaebikkyin to Mogok road, further to the south, or turn due east to cross the Mongmit to Mogok road before turning south again to head for the Gokteik. We crossed the Nabu to Mongmit track on the night of 26 March and pushed on with all speed, the decision having been taken to turn east and cross the Mongmit to Mogok road before turning to the south. Once again we crossed a major hazard in darkness and we found a safe bivouac in thick jungle several miles to the east of the road. By this time we were all exhausted, for we had been on the move with very little rest for the previous 24 hours. Physically, most of us were at a very low ebb by this time. Tough though the Gurkhas and BURRIFS were, they too were beginning to suffer. We all needed a period of rest on adequate rations, untroubled by the possibility of enemy action. It was not to be, as the crisis point of the whole operation would soon be upon us.

During the night of 27 March we received a signal from Brigade Headquarters cancelling the proposed operation against the Gokteik Viaduct. I learned later that the reason for this cancellation was that we and No 3 Column would have been out of range of supply-dropping flights by the time we reached the area of our objective. It seemed that the available Dakota aircraft did not have the fuel capacity to ensure a successful return flight. When I heard this, I remember wondering why they could not have thought of this *before* we started the agonizing march southwards from Nam Pan Chaung. The same signal informed us that Wingate had decided the time had come to return to "friendly" territory. I believe the deterioration in the health of the soldiers in every Column and the knowledge that the Brigade was virtually hemmed in by the Japanese were the two major factors which brought about this decision. It seemed that the party was over. Our last supply drop had been on 21 March and it was now a week later. As a consequence we had little food left in reserve and a bumper drop was requested so that we would all have as much as we could carry. This was vital as, if we split up into small parties of up to forty strong, each party would march back by a different route to avoid major clashes with the enemy. In this case there would be no wireless to demand more supplies and each party would be on its own and would have to fend for itself. I learned that dispersal of Columns into small parties had been well practised during the months of training in the Central Provinces of India before the Brigade had moved to

Burma, and this was clearly a possible option now. A signal demanding this important supply drop was sent on 28 March. The drop was scheduled for 30 March, at a DZ which had been selected as suitable by Flight Lieutenant Edmunds and was some five miles to the south-east of our present location.

At this time there was considerable discussion about possible routes for our return to friendly territory. The majority view seemed to be that, in spite of the distance and the two major river obstacles – first the Irrawaddy and then the Chindwin – it would be preferable to go back by roughly the same route we had taken for the outward trek. If possible we should not re-enter the Shweli Triangle but should cross the Irrawaddy somewhere between Tagaung in the north and Thabeikkyin in the south. We should then head westwards for a crossing of the Chindwin somewhere between Paungbyin and Auktaung. This would require a march in excess of 250 miles, as with the outward journey. Colonel Alex and Major Dunlop also gave much consideration to the alternative of marching eastwards into China. The snag with this option was that, although the frontier with Yunnan Province was less than 150 miles from us at its nearest point, we did not know how far the Japanese had penetrated into Yunnan, nor did we have any worthwhile information about the Chinese forces in this area. I had listened to most of these discussions and I understood that the general feeling was "better the devil you know" – a return march westwards to India was more favoured than the China option.

Early on 29 March Colonel Alex sent me out on a minor patrol task. Most of the Reconnaissance Platoon were out at this time, making sure that the country around the selected DZ for the next vital supply drop was clear of the enemy for a radius of at least four miles in all directions. My task was to return to a point overlooking the Mogok to Mongmit road, close to where we had crossed the road on the night of 27 March. I was to observe the frequency of enemy patrols in vehicles and on foot and the extent and direction of troop movements along the road during the next 24 hours. I was then to report back, with my observations, to him at HQ 1 Group before nightfall on 30 March and at the location of the supply drop that had been arranged for the afternoon of that day. This would entail a short march of 3 to 4 miles to reach the road and a return march of 8 to 9 miles to reach the location of the DZ. The jungle was fairly thick and there were hills to contend with but I was confident that we could do the job and cover the distances involved in the time available.

I had with me a BURRIF Havildar (Sergeant) with whom I had worked on a number of previous patrols. His name was Aung Hla and in these circumstances I could not have asked for a better SNCO. He was a Karen, considerably older than I (probably about 33 years old), and a very experienced soldier who had come out of Burma with the 1942 retreat. He spoke good English and was completely loyal and supportive. In addition, there were three BURRIF riflemen, one a Karen and two Kachins. The patrol was made up to a total of twelve (including myself) by the addition of a Naik (Corporal) and six riflemen from 3/2 GR. The Gurkha Naik had also been with me on a previous patrol. I am sure one of his names was Gurung but I cannot remember his first name. Each of us carried our personal weapons and in our packs rations for three days in addition to our standard emergency rations and all our normal allocation of ammunition, grenades and personal gear.

We made good time to the road, arriving there at about 11 am, and selected a vantage point on a small ridge from which we had a good view down on to the road during daylight, while being well concealed by the jungle around us. I posted Gurkhas in pairs as sentries to the north, south and east of our position, the BURRIF's stayed with me at the observation point and our Gurkha Naik did the rounds periodically to each of the pairs of Gurkha sentries. During the afternoon I went down closer to the road, with great caution and with one of the Kachin riflemen as my "pair", to select a good vantage point for observation after darkness fell. It was a long 24 hours and we noted a considerable number of trucks (I forget the exact figure), apparently filled with Japanese soldiers, travelling northwards from Mogok towards Mongmit. Very few vehicles passed in the other direction and we saw no foot patrols during our 24 hours of observation. It seemed that the Japanese were continuing to reinforce their attempt to put a stranglehold on the Shweli Triangle to the north of us.

49

My orders had been to watch the road for 24 hours. By noon on 30 March we had withdrawn from the ridge overlooking the road and were on our way back to join up with HQ 1 Group and No 1 Column at the location chosen for the supply drop that had been arranged for that afternoon. I hoped that my report would be of some value to Colonel Alex and was anxious to rejoin the Column as quickly as possible. We made good progress at first and in less than two hours had reached the area where I had left them on the previous day. There was no sign of their presence and they had covered their tracks on leaving with the expertise that I had come to accept as normal. We rested for ten minutes or so and then marched on by compass bearing towards the location I had been given for the DZ. The terrain became more and more difficult as we progressed, with thick jungle and some steep hills to negotiate. After about an hour of struggling we came across a small stream, too small to call a chaung but which provided us with water to fill our chaguls. By this time it was after 3 pm and in the distance we heard the drone of Dakota aircraft, although we did not see them because of the jungle overhang above us. The aircraft noise did not last long and I began to wonder whether the drop had been aborted, as we could only have been a few miles from the DZ at this time. A short time later we thought we heard the sound of small arms fire in the distance but we could not be sure of this. Nevertheless from this time on we proceeded more slowly and with great caution. As we neared the area I believed to be the location selected for the DZ my Gurkhas disappeared into the jungle on my instructions to search the area to our flanks and try to make contact with the Column. After an hour or so they had all returned, having drawn a blank. I then moved forward myself, on the compass bearing, with Aung Hla and the three BURRIF riflemen, leaving the Gurkhas to rest. I also had no success and, as by this time the darkness of night was approaching, we rejoined the Gurkhas and made a safe bivouac in the thick jungle, determined to seek out and rejoin the Column at dawn next day.

The search for our comrades was resumed next morning as soon as it was light enough for the task. Within half an hour we came to an area on top of a low wide ridge along which the jungle was much less thick. We closed up to this area with great care and I soon realized that we had found the DZ location. We found no indication that a drop had taken place but I had no doubt that the Column had been there. Unusually, we found signs of a hasty departure, for it was evident that the final clear-up had not been carried out with the customary thoroughness and efficiency. We found some discarded rubbish, some mule droppings and the cold remnants of several fires. We had arrived at the correct location but we were more than 12 hours later than planned because of our enforced bivouac during the darkness of the previous night. It was my guess that the Column had received information during the previous afternoon, most probably from reconnaissance by the BURRIFS, of an approaching Japanese force. This would have resulted in a decision to abort the drop and to leave the area immediately. No doubt the Column would arrange another supply drop in a few days time at another location, but we had no idea where this would be. The next step was to try to track the Column by looking for signs of their movement from this DZ, but, in spite of the signs of hasty departure, our friends had applied their jungle-craft with the usual skill and every track we followed petered out in thick jungle. We searched for two or three hours with great care as we realized that Japs might still be in the area, but to no avail. Slowly it dawned on me that we would never find them. They might be anywhere, might soon be dividing up into smaller parties and we had no idea which route any of these parties would be taking in an attempt to return to India. I can remember all the events leading up to this realization of our situation, for it was a traumatic experience.

We were on our own.

I realized that, if we were to get out safely and survive, it would be up to me and to Aung Hla and our Gurkha Naik. I remembered the lesson that had been rammed home to us as officer cadets by David Horsfield, our Chief Instructor at Mhow: "In crisis, don't panic; *never* show anxiety or lack of confidence to the men for whom you are responsible; even when the bottom seems to have fallen out of your world, keep your head and behave as though everything is under control; then consider all the factors, make a decision and get on with it." Now, for the first time in my limited experience, I was faced with a real crisis. In fact, our

51

survival and eventual safe return to India was due not so much to myself, Aung Hla and the Naik but more to the two BURRIF Kachin riflemen with us, for this was their country. All I had to do was to make the decision to go for China rather than a return direct to India by our long outward route across Burma. From then on their help and local knowledge got us out. Without them I doubt that we could have made it.

I made the decision to head for the Yunnan Province of China after much discussion with Aung Hla. We considered all the possible options only after a very careful listing of our limited assets and our limitations. The first thing I checked was the ration state. We were all in weak physical shape but could still march through this difficult terrain. How long this would last would depend largely upon the availability of food and water to keep us going. All the Gurkhas and BURRIFS carried a small sack of rice in their packs. In addition, we all had our normal ration for three days, consisting of Shakapura biscuits (a square wholemeal biscuit), blocks of compressed raisins and nuts, compressed dates, a small quantity of cheese, salt, tea, sugar, powdered milk, acid drops and some 'V' (for Victory!) cigarettes. All these were the normal ration and we had been living on them for weeks by this time. We had learned early on that the Shakapura biscuits, the raisins and the nuts could be made into a sort of hot porridge to vary the boredom of feeding constantly on this nutritious but monotonous fare. (We had each gone in for "self-catering" from the start, heating our own food in our mess tins. There was no communal cooking on "LONG-CLOTH".) Occasionally an exciting and unexpected bonus had come down in a supply drop and I remember I had safely tucked away, in the bottom of my pack, one tin of peaches and one tin of bully beef. My check on all twelve of us revealed that we carried between us enough food to keep us going for four or five days, or a week at most if we went on to much reduced rations. I also found that, between them, our seven Gurkhas had three degchis (small round metal cooking pots), which were a boon as our mess-tins were by now falling apart due to constant use, over individual little fires, to heat water for the essential daily drinks of hot tea. We also had some malted milk tablets and a good supply of atebrin tablets to keep malaria at bay. Equally vital to our well being was an adequate supply of water. Each of us carried a small stock of water sterilizing tablets and each of us had a chagul which we had filled from the stream on our way back from the standing patrol at the road. The chagul was a canvas sack, shaped with an almost oval main body and with a long narrow neck, which we dangled from the side of our packs with the spout pointing upwards. Although the outside of the chagul always seemed to be damp, the water did not leak away but rather became cooler the more the sun shone upon it.

None of this altered the fact that we would only be able to keep going for a week or so. After that we would have to find food. Going back the way we had come would mean a trek of at least 250 miles over country the inhabitants of which were not all of a friendly disposition. I thought also that the Japanese would expect the Brigade to return by marching back the way we had come and that therefore the likelihood of encounters with the enemy would be far greater than if we marched east into China. In addition, we knew that the nearest point of Yunnan Province from our present position was between 100 and 150 miles away, as opposed to the 250 miles or more we would have to cover to return to the River Chindwin.

But there was one other factor which made the decision to march east into China the obvious and only sensible solution. The two BURRIF Kachins who were with us knew this part of Burma well. One came from a village which was south of the upper Shweli and not far from a place called Man Na, which was fairly near to the frontier. The other came from a village in the Kachin Hills to the south of the Sinlumkaba Hill Tracts. Havildar Aung Hla talked with them and questioned them in detail, his 'Jinghpaw' (the language of the Kachins) being much better than the attempts at spoken English made by the two Kachins. He then assured me that the Kachin rifleman who came from the hills to the east of us, beyond the Kodaung Hill Tracts, could probably find food for us from one of the villages in his home area. He also believed that from then on we had good hopes of a guide to show us the way north-eastwards across the upper Shweli and either into the area known to our other Kachin or onward directly into Yunnan. The one essential would be to avoid contact with the Japanese and to minimize the possibility of news of our existence reaching them. It followed that only our two Kachins, and possibly Aung Hla, would go into any village we came across and then only in civilian clothes. (They all carried loongyis in their packs; these were a sort of long wrap-over skirt-type garment worn by most men in Burma, with a loose shirt-type top.) The rest of us would wait in the jungle outside villages and hope that the negotiations would produce something to eat. Before coming in to Burma all officers and SNCOs had been given a small number of silver coins to carry for just such an emergency, so that purchases could be made for cash. I had missed this hand-out because of my late arrival to join the Brigade, but Aung Hla still had his issue intact and this proved to be very useful during the next few weeks.

The decision having been made, we left the area of the DZ and marched for a few miles towards the east, taking great care to cover our tracks so that we would not be followed by any inquisitive Japanese, should they be around. We then settled into a safe bivouac in thick jungle. From this night on we established a routine of having two sentries awake and alert at any time while the rest were sleeping in a bivouac. This meant that every other night each of us spent three hours on picquet duty while the other ten could rest and in this way on every alternate night six of us could have an undisturbed rest. The system worked well and, although for most of the next three weeks we were all utterly exhausted at the end of each day's march, none of the twelve of us ever let the others down by falling asleep during their three-hour spells of picquet duty. That first evening I worked out with Havildar Aung Hla, and with the help of the only (somewhat tattered) map I had with me, a compass bearing towards Man Na on which we would march until our Kachin recognized the area near a village that he knew. At dawn next morning we left our bivouac and began the march into the Kodaung Hill Tracts. An agonizing trek lay ahead of us, which eventually led us to safety.

It took us eight days to reach a village known to our BURRIF Kachin rifleman. By this time we were all desperately hungry, the last of our meagre rations had gone and we were in poor physical shape. Our Kachin returned to us with some rice, some cooked chicken and goat meat and a guide. He told Aung Hla that no Japanese had been seen in the village for some months. The guide was the first living soul we had seen since leaving our standing patrol position on the Mogok to Mongmit road ten days before. Before leaving, Aung Hla himself went into the village with the guide and purchased some more rice. When they returned, Aung Hla assured me that the guide had promised to take us across the Upper Shweli valley to the north and onwards to a village where he would try to find another guide for the march north-eastwards into Yunnan. We had to put our trust in him and he kept his word. From now on we lived mainly on rice (and the water in which the rice had been boiled) and there were days when we had nothing. A day or two after taking food from the first village we had reached I began to show all the signs of having contracted dysentery. This condition stayed with me for the remainder of the march out and added greatly to my other personal troubles, which included the jungle sores on my shins and what, from the yellow of my skin and whites of my eyes, I took to be jaundice.

The next two weeks became a struggle to keep going and survive. My memories of this awful period are extremely vague. I remember a succession of agonizing marches through jungle and up and down very steep slopes by day and the complete exhaustion felt in each bivouac – and especially I remember the fight against and the fear of sleep on those occasions when it was my turn for three hours on picquet duty. Physically we all began to fade as the days went by and during the last week I am sure I was in the hands of my Karen, Kachin and Gurkha comrades rather than the reverse. They shared my determination to get out to safety, kept cheerful and alert, and looked after me and my welfare as best they could in the circumstances, when really it should have been I who looked after them. We had a succession of guides from several villages on our way and, having crossed the upper Shweli from the south, we turned north-eastwards and followed the river valley towards Yunnan. We kept well to the north of the river itself and eventually reached a tributary called the River Longchuan, which joined the Shweli from the north. We kept well clear of a place with the same name as the tributary because, although this was in Yunnan, we did not know whether we were still in territory occupied by the Japanese.

55

Somehow or other (and with the help of my Gurkhas) I managed to keep going until we reached the road near a small town called Longling, where we suddenly found ourselves in the hands of the Chinese Army. Our last guide had left us before this and Havildar Aung Hla was really responsible for taking us on this last day's march which brought us to safety. I was told by him that by this time I was rather delirious. I remember little except for the blessed relief of a ride in a Chinese Army truck to a place of some size called Baoshan. My companions had somehow scrounged a stretcher for me and I remember little more until I found myself on the floor of a cargo-carrying Dakota aircraft of the US Air Force, with all my companions squatting around me as we took off from the Baoshan airstrip for the flight "over the Hump" and back to India. I am proud to say that we still had all our personal weapons and equipment with us, although our marching boots were beginning to fall apart at the seams. In any event, we were out. It was over.

We landed first at an airfield near to Dibrugarh in Northern Assam. Sadly, I parted company there with my companions who had been loyal and devoted comrades in times of adversity. I believe they were sent on to a Field Hospital at Imphal. I tried to trace them later but without success. I also did my utmost to ensure that Havildar Aung Hla received some form of recognition for all he had done but I heard nothing more and fear that my recommendations fell on deaf ears. I was flown from Dibrugarh to Dum Dum (Calcutta) in a Royal Air Force transport plane and eventually ended up at the Base Hospital in Ranchi (I was to be a patient there again two years later). By now it was 28 April 1943 and I was to spend the next six or seven weeks in hospital and convalescence. I had lost three stone in weight during Operation "LONGCLOTH" and was very ill when I arrived at Ranchi. The excellent medical treatment and nursing given to me at the Base Hospital began to produce positive results in a remarkably short space of time. The dysentery responded to the drugs I was given and soon I was able to start eating properly again. As a result I began to put on some weight, to overcome the drastic effects of malnutrition. The jungle sores also responded to treatment and, with constant changes of dressings and the application of a mysterious yellow powder, soon began to heal. As to my jaundiced appearance, this too began to fade away as the weeks went by. Later in life, when I was in my late fifties, modern and sophisticated X-ray equipment revealed that (in the words of my doctors): "There was evidence of the scars of self-healing of a massive microbial infestation of the liver, which probably occurred in the early adult life of the patient". I believe it is probable that my experiences during the latter stages of Operation "LONGCLOTH" may have been responsible for this.

After a month in the hospital at Ranchi I was given three weeks' convalescent leave in Srinagar. I left Ranchi on 28 May 1943, which was my twentieth birthday. This was my first visit to Kashmir and I arrived two days later, after a long rail and road journey. I was somewhat overwhelmed by the beauty of the Himalayas and the Vale of Kashmir. The welcome and kindness I received from M, who took me into her house as though it was my home, was also quite overwhelming. She was a most charming and attractive woman, about eight years older than I, whose husband had been killed while serving with his Indian Army battalion in the Middle East in 1941. Her home was off the Raj Bagh, close to Dal Lake on the outskirts of Srinagar, and she (and many other householders there) had volunteered to take in and look after convalescent servicemen. For three weeks I was nursed, fed and spoilt to such an extent that my return to normality and fitness was swift and sure. Needless to say, it did not take too long for me to fall in love with my hostess and this first visit to Kashmir was the beginning of a love affair which lasted until after the end of the War in 1945. I was to spend every leave (sick leave or otherwise) during the next 2½ years with M at her home in Srinagar and I came to look upon her house as my home in India. At first her attitude to me was one of sympathy and caring but, in due course, she also fell in love, in spite of our age difference. These brief periods of leave in Kashmir were islands of happiness which perhaps did more than anything else to keep me sane and on an even keel during the madness of the war in Burma.

During those idyllic three weeks I had time to reflect on Operation "LONGCLOTH" and my own very meagre contribution. To my great surprise the Operation was given enormous publicity and the newspapers seemed to be treating us as heroes. At first I tended to bask in all this attention, but after a while I found myself indulging in a little self-examination and came to two conclusions. Firstly, I personally had contributed very little to the success of the enterprise. I had just followed on with the others and had not even seen the enemy face to face. I had learned a great deal about the jungles and countryside of Upper Burma and how to survive in these jungles, but there was little more that I could claim. Secondly, I came to doubt that the whole operation had been worthwhile. 3,000 of us went in and I was to learn that only 2,000 came out. It seemed that all we had done was to kill a small number of the enemy, blow up the railway in a few places (damage which could be repaired in a matter of weeks), and cock a snook at the Japanese for the first time by marching a large body of men across Burma and back. But I began to ask myself whether it was worthwhile to lose a third of our number to achieve such limited results and gain some experience of "what it was like in there". I was very proud to have taken part in the enterprise but I was not to feel that I was properly earning my pay until my participation in the horrors of the Imphal Siege a year later. In the near future I was to learn with much sadness that my mentor, Colonel Alex, Lieutenant Colonel L.A. Alexander, 3/2 GR, had been posted as "Missing, believed killed" during the march out, after I had lost contact with him. Flight Lieutenant Edmunds was also missing and Spurlock, the Brigade Signal Officer I had never met, had been left behind in the jungle, too ill to march on with Wingate and his small party. I heard also that Aung Hla's Commanding Officer, Lieutenant Colonel L.G. Wheeler, had been shot dead by the Japanese in early April at a small village called Zibyugin, and realized how this news would devastate the Burma Rifles and the Kachin and Karen tribes. I began to realize how fortunate I had been and to question again whether such tragic waste had been worthwhile. I asked myself why we had gone into Burma in the first place and what was the purpose of Operation "LONGCLOTH". I was to learn much later that the original concept had been for our Columns to get far behind the enemy facing our forces on the Chindwin. We were to attack their Lines of Communication and disrupt their rear areas as a coordinated effort with our main forces based on Imphal, which were to go onto the offensive as soon as we were in place deep inside Burma. Unfortunately the main offensive had to be called off at the last moment and a decision had to be made at high level as to whether or not our Long Range Penetration operation should go ahead. Apparently Wingate had persuaded Wavell (who had come to Imphal to see us on our way) that "LONGCLOTH" should proceed as planned. Wingate's main argument was that 77 Brigade was at the very peak of readiness after long, hard and careful training. He maintained that to cancel at the last moment would have the effect of deflating the *esprit de corps* of the Brigade to such an extent that our effectiveness as a fighting formation would be permanently damaged. Wingate's arguments were accepted and we went in as planned, but without the offensive by IV Corps (17 and 23 Indian Divisions) which had been the primary reason for going in the first place. There was to have been an offensive into Burma from Yunnan by the Chinese at the same time but this also was cancelled, so we went in on our own. I knew nothing of this until long after I had returned to India but when I heard the background story I began to understand "the reason why". I also heard stories that our Southern Group was considered by Wingate to be expendable and had been abandoned by him in the later stages of the Operation, our deception task having been completed. I do not know the truth of this but I certainly felt we had been abandoned when I found myself alone with my small patrol in the jungle to the east of the Mogok to Mongmit road on 31 March 1943.

My three weeks of convalescence in Kashmir came to an end far too quickly. I said my goodbyes to M, with promises that I would be back if she would have me and expressions of gratitude which seemed to be quite inadequate. My orders were to proceed to Meerut, where I would be given further instructions. I travelled down to Rawalpindi by hire car and thence by train to Meerut, where I was told to take up my original posting and join 111 Infantry Brigade Signal Section. I understood that I would be required to attend a Medical Board at some time after my arrival at 111 Brigade. It seemed that the Brigade (which was the second Chindit Brigade and had been forming while we in 77 Brigade were in Burma on Operation "LONGCLOTH") was now undergoing jungle training and was located at a place called Ghatera in the jungles of the Central Provinces. I searched for Ghatera on the map but could not find it.

My railway warrant was made out to the place but "Movements" at Meerut told me to travel to a small town called Lalitpur, between Jhansi and Saugor, and ask for directions when I got there. I still had some of my personal kit from "LONGCLOTH" but had been provided with all the replacements that I needed by the stores organization at Meerut. When I arrived at Lalitpur, I was put on to a goods train which travelled down a single-track line and eventually reached a siding in the middle of the jungle, which turned out to be all there was of a place called Ghatera! The Brigade Headquarters and the Signal Section were in the jungle a short drive by jeep from the railway siding.

I reported to my new Officer Commanding, whose name was Captain S.O. Briggs. In fact, he was my first Royal Signals OC, as I had never met Spurlock in 77 Brigade. Briggs greeted me without enthusiasm and, even on short acquaintance, we did not hit it off. He was a wartime soldier who had been a Customs Officer in peacetime. I learned that he had come out of Burma in the 1942 retreat, serving under the command of Major David Horsfield with HQ Burma Corps. As soon as I had found a tent and had dumped my kit I was introduced to Brigadier W.D.A. (Joe) Lentaigne, DSO, my new Brigade Commander. He was older than I had expected, a tall angular man with tanned, pointed features and spectacles. His whole manner commanded respect and he greeted me pleasantly enough, but it was evident that his mind was on other things. After all, I was just another subaltern joining his Brigade. I also met his Brigade Major, Jack Masters. He had quite a different personality and I took to him immediately. He had a good sense of humour, but was quick, decisive and very much on the ball. He was, of course, the same Jack (John) Masters who became the famous author of many best-selling books after the war. Both he and the Brigadier were pre-war regular officers from Gurkha infantry regiments.

I settled in to my new surroundings and began to become involved with the intensive training of the Brigade. The two infantry battalions with which I had most contact were the 4/9 Gurkha Rifles and the 1st Cameronians (Scottish Rifles), the latter being a hard-bitten lot of extremely tough soldiers who had already fought the Japanese during the 1942 retreat. My job now was the more conventional one of being second-in-command of the Brigade Signal Section. I was anxious to prove that I was fit again and able to cope with the job. Perhaps I was too anxious to prove myself but I found I had little support from Briggs, who seemed to regard my enthusiasm with a certain amount of amusement and contempt. After a week or so Brigadier Joe Lentaigne took me to one side and told me that he did not think I would be able to recover my full physical fitness in time to go back into action in Burma with the Brigade. He also told me quite frankly that he felt I was too young to be involved in Long Range Penetration operations, in spite of my experiences on Operation "LONGCLOTH". As can be imagined, this interview with Joe Lentaigne upset me greatly and I was determined to prove him wrong by redoubling my efforts during the training. Then two disasters, which occurred one after the other in a week, sealed my fate. The first was an endurance march ordered by Briggs. I took most of the soldiers of the Signal Section on a forced march of 12 miles through the jungle in 2½ hours. I was determined to show that I myself was fit enough to do this and I managed it, although I was completely exhausted when we returned to camp; but not all the soldiers I took with me on this march were as fit as I. After about an hour of fast marching in the heat of the day one of my men (he was an Instrument Mechanic by trade) told me that he was feeling ill. I told him to sit in the shade and detailed another man to stay with him and help him back to camp when he felt well enough to move. I and the others marched on at a fast pace. When we reached camp, there was no sign of the two men. A search party was sent out and one man was found dead from heatstroke and the other (the one I had detailed to look after him) was found unconscious by his side. I felt like a murderer and blamed myself for this tragedy. Briggs gave me little support and I could not help feeling that the men of the Signal Section now regarded me as a hard and brutal young officer. Later, when they went into Burma for the first time with the second Wingate expedition in

1944, I fear they all experienced very much harder forced marches than this little test of their endurance which had ended in such a tragic way.

The second disaster was so complete that it ended my time with the Chindits. After only a few weeks with 111 Brigade at Ghatera, I was beset with the most agonizing pain in my right abdomen. I was suffering from acute appendicitis and was carried from the jungle training area to the railway siding by four Gurkhas of 4/9 GR. It was early July 1943.

Chapter 4

INTERLUDE ON THE NORTH-WEST FRONTIER
AUGUST 1943 TO JANUARY 1944

They took me from Ghatera on a stretcher. For me, this form of transport was becoming synonymous with LRPG. It seemed that I ended each phase of my time with Wingate's Special Force by being carted off on a stretcher and (eventually) into hospital. My departure from 111 Infantry Brigade Signal Section, Special Force, was so soon after my arrival there from sick leave, following "LONGCLOTH" and my time with 77 Brigade, that I had hardly had time to settle down under my new OC, Captain Briggs, Joe Lentaigne, my new Brigadier, and Jack Masters, the Brigade Major. As it turned out, I was not to return to the Chindits. Perhaps this was my good luck, although I did not think so at the time. At least by now I was a full Lieutenant, with two pips on each shoulder.

I remember little of my departure from the Brigade, nor of the journey to Jubbulpore, for I was in such pain that my knees seemed to be firmly fixed to my chest with the agony of my appendix (which I learned later was about to burst). Soon after my arrival at the Military Hospital I was on the operating table. I awoke some time after this to find that I had a 3½ inch wound on the right-hand side of my lower abdomen, duly stitched together with what looked like blanket stitches and with a drain pipe sticking out above it. The Indian Medical Service looked after me well and, after some weeks of nursing and the realization that it had been a near thing, for peritonitis is not really a subject for hilarity, I was once again sent on sick leave.

Inevitably I returned to Srinagar, and to M, the woman who had helped me to regain my health and strength after "LONG-CLOTH". I was beginning to believe that I was desperately in love with her, but then I was only 20 years old and this had never happened to me before. Perhaps at this stage she was just sorry for me, for it was the second time in as many months that she had looked after me when I was in such poor physical shape. She cared for me in the same way as before and, in due course, I was called before a Medical Board in Rawalpindi. After this, I was told that I had been medically down-graded and would not be permitted to return to active service in Burma for five months, and then only if a further Medical Board passed me as completely fit.

Meanwhile I was posted from Rawalpindi to Waziristan District Signals, in the North-West Frontier Province. I left Rawalpindi by train for Mari-Indus, where I crossed the River Indus by ferry, to be met and driven to Dehra Ismail Khan (DIK) by jeep from Waziristan District Signals. On arrival, I reported myself to the adjutant and was told to present myself to the Commanding Officer, Lt Col Beeton, at 9 am the next morning. The Colonel greeted me affably enough but it soon became clear that he disapproved of "funnies" such as LRPG. I heard later that he had written, in the Confidential Report of an officer he disliked, the following revealing comment: "This officer wishes to volunteer for Long Range Penetration Groups. As far as I am concerned, the longer the penetration the better"! In any event, he informed me that he had decided to post me to Bannu Brigade Signal Section as second-in-command. A few months with a Brigade Section on the Frontier, under the command of Captain Paddy Roy, would help me to learn something about soldiering in a properly conducted unit. It would also help me to grow up and forget about the unorthodox ways of waging war that had undoubtedly been forced upon me while with Wingate's private army. I made no comment and accepted my fate. To push the lesson home, the Colonel terminated the interview by informing me that I would be required to assume the duties of Headquarters Orderly Officer for the next week to "help me gain experience". I was then to move to Bannu by road and report to Captain Paddy Roy for duties as his 2IC.

I duly carried out my long, and somewhat unfair, stint of Orderly Officer at HQ Waziristan District. The duties were quite onerous. I recall that I had to inspect the security of arms in the Armoury four times each 24 hours. The bolts of all rifles were kept under lock and key quite separately from the rifles themselves, which were padlocked and chained to fixtures in the armoury walls. This was because the hostile tribesmen, although able to make a perfectly functional copy of the standard Lee-Enfield rifle (which was then the basic personal weapon of the British and Indian infantryman), did not have the tools nor the expertise to manufacture the bolt. They were known to have small arms factories in caves in the mountains but sent out thieves (usually young boys) to steal bolts from the armouries of British and Indian Army units.

The Headquarters of Waziristan District, which was similar in organization to a divisional headquarters and included the bulk of Waziristan Signals, was housed in a large "Beau Geste" type fortification and my duties included the guarding, security and regular inspection of a large part of this collection of buildings. It was necessary for me to be out and about throughout each night. As a consequence, I had little sleep during my week of duty. This was soldiering old style and no doubt the routines I had to follow had been in operation without much change since the previous century. How different this was from life during Operation "LONGCLOTH" in Burma. Here our turnout had to be immaculate, with starched khaki drill shorts and shirts, highly polished Sam Browne belt and boots, and with hosetops, puttees and khaki solar topee, bright with cleanliness with the Signals colours in a patch on the left-hand side and worn straight over the eyes. A loaded hand-gun (a .38 revolver) was carried at all times. Short haircuts were *de rigueur*. Although I had already been a commissioned officer for over six months and was now a full Lieutenant (albeit temporary), this was my first experience of the formality of peacetime soldiering and the rigid discipline and strict adherence to a set pattern of life that was typical of the pre-war Indian Army. There was much to be said for it but it took some time for me to adjust and settle down. After all, I had been thrown straight into Wingate's first expedition into Burma as soon as I had emerged from the Officer Cadet Training Unit at Mhow. Since then I had either been marching, day in and day out, in Japanese-held territory through Northern Burma to China or had been in hospital followed by sick leave. As a consequence, my experience as a commissioned officer in a normal unit was virtually nil, although I had received my first hard lessons in the survival techniques needed when fighting the Japanese. My new CO, Colonel Beeton, was quite right. I needed to learn a great deal about the other side of soldiering, to forget for the moment the Special Force attitudes and get down to the nuts and bolts of being a young subaltern in a normal unit.

During this first week I was allocated a bearer, my personal servant who was to look after my every need. He was a Punjabi youth, about 16 years old, and seemed pleasant and helpful, although still learning his job. His wage was the equivalent in rupees of 25 shillings (one pound 25p nowadays) per *month*, and this was the accepted going rate for bearers at that time! As it happened and through no fault of his own, he was only my bearer for a few days.

At the end of my first week in DIK I received formal orders to move. A 30 cwt truck was allocated to take me, my bearer and my kit (which now included a metal uniform trunk), by road to Bannu. Since my destination was on the borders of hostile tribal territory and as the road from DIK went through the Pezu Pass (which was in tribal territory and could only be used when the road was "open" and protected by infantry pickets), there was a rule that travellers had to be through and clear of the Pass before 2 pm each day. We set off early in the morning, with plenty of time in hand, but the truck broke down before we reached the Pass and we were delayed for two hours or more before we got the engine going again. As time was now short, although I felt sure we could get through the Pass before 2 pm, I decided to drive the vehicle myself, putting the Indian driver (he was a Madrassi) in the passenger seat beside me. I drove fast, we reached and passed through Pezu with time to spare and then, during the home run to Bannu, disaster struck. I was a very inexperienced driver (although I held a valid Army licence) and, when the truck developed a front wheel skid in sand that had been blown onto the tarmac by the wind, I over-corrected. The result was a series of skids, first one way and then the other, in more loose sand over the road, until eventually the truck turned over twice and ended up on its side. Although considerably shaken, neither I nor the driver were hurt, but my bearer, riding in the back of the vehicle, had been badly mauled by my metal trunk as the truck, he and the trunk revolved. Later that afternoon the crashed vehicle was recovered, my bearer was taken to hospital and the driver and I arrived at last in Bannu in a manner not recommended when reporting for duty for the first time in a new unit. Paddy Roy, my new OC, was philosophical about it all and hastily convened a Court of Inquiry, which somehow absolved me from blame and produced the verdict "Act of God – State to pay!" This, then, was my introduction to Bannu Brigade Signal Section and Captain Paddy Roy.

I soon discovered that Bannu was an interesting station, much sought after as a posting "on the Frontier". This was because, although in hostile tribal territory, it was the only "family" station in tribal Waziristan. As a consequence, Bannu offered a social life that was quite extraordinary for the North West Frontier. All the officers with accompanying wives and families, who were serving in "male-only" forts such as Miranshah, Wana, Gardai, Razmak and other defended localities close to the border with Afghanistan, had to leave their womenfolk in Bannu. For this reason Bannu was one of those very rare Army stations in India where there seemed to be more women than men. This, of course, was not the case but it seemed to be that way! There was an Officers' Club, with tennis courts, a delightful swimming-pool, bars and billiards rooms and where dances and other social events seemed to be the norm. There was also a Military Hospital with a full quota of Nursing Sisters and Nurses, so that female company was not all that difficult to find.

Putting to one side this exciting prospect, something so unusual in India that it was difficult to believe, I soon found that there was work to be done. We were not in Bannu just to enjoy ourselves! For me, this was a new world, entirely different from the war in Burma. We seemed to have moved back to soldiering in the last century. It was all deadly serious, for the

67

tribesman's "bandook" could kill just as finally as a modern weapon, but it was difficult to understand the point of it all when a world war was being fought for survival of ourselves and our way of life, not only against the Nazis, who seemed so far away, but also against the Japanese barbarians much closer to us on the India/Burma border.

The country on the Frontier was arid and mountainous with very little vegetation. The tribesmen in the villages up to and over the frontier with Afghanistan led an impoverished existence, for there was little chance of growing crops in the dry, rocky soil of the mountains, and they seemed to find enjoyment mainly from feuds between villages and tribes, as they were frequently fighting and killing one another. Another favourite sport was the practice of shooting at us (and sometimes killing one of us). This was the area where, in pre-war days, the notorious Fakir of Ipi had succeeded in persuading a number of different tribes to join forces in a revolt which became a running sore for some years to the British and Indian soldiers on the Frontier and also to the Government of British India. I found that there was an extraordinary practice of payments by the Government to troublesome villages or tribes, so that they could be punished by suspension of all or part of these payments should the village or tribe concerned become too troublesome to us. From time to time long columns of tribesmen, Wazirs, Pathans, Tochis, Mahsoods, Afridis, and others, riding or leading heavily laden camels, would come down from the mountains in single file and pass by or through Bannu on their way into India to sell their wares. They all seemed to carry firearms, usually long bandooks, some of which looked like home-made weapons made from metal pipes with flintlock firing mechanisms, and others which looked suspiciously like our Lee-Enfield rifles. The tribesmen were permitted to carry firearms at all times and I found it difficult to understand how we were expected to differentiate between those of friendly disposition and the "dushman" (enemy). Most wore pugris, which were made into a rough turban by winding a long strip of dirty white cloth around the head, and they were usually swathed in somewhat dirty white loose apparel under which any additional weapon could have been concealed. Yet it seemed that few

1. The Officer Training School, Bangalore, April 1942. The author, recumbent, relaxing between lectures with two fellow cadets.

2. Operation Longcloth, February 1943. Wavell bids farewell to Southern Group at Imphal before the march into Burma. Lt-Colonel L.A. Alexander, Commanding 3/2 Gurkha Rifles and No.1 Group, is on the right with his back to the camera. (*Imperial War Museum*)

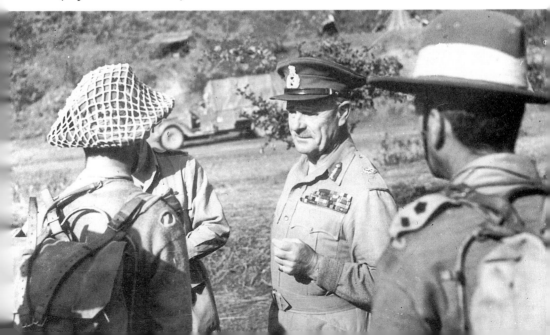

3. Operation Longcloth. Calling for a supply drop. (*Imperial War Museum*)

4. Operation Longcloth. Co-ordination by wireless while crossing the Chindwin when outward bound. (*Imperial War Museum*)

5. Operation Longcloth, March 1943. Wingate deep in enemy territory. (*Imperial War Museum*)

6. III (Chindit) Brigade, June 1943, at Ghatera. The author's "pair" and personal orderly, Bhagurat Singh, with Tommy gun. Note jungle behind him.

7. The Siege of Imphal, April - June 1944. "Scraggy" on Shenam Ridge. Note destroyed bunkers and obliteration of the jungle which once covered the hill. (*Imperial War Museum*)

8. Imphal. Nippon Hill, overlooking all our positions on Shenam Ridge; a thorn in our sides for three months and a Battle Honour, at terrible cost, for the 1st Bn, the Devonshire Regiment. (*Imperial War Museum*)

9. Imphal. A British mortar team in action. Mortars proved most effective weapons in jungle warfare. (*Imperial War Museum*)

10. Imphal: Shenam Ridge, July - August 1944. Japanese dead being cremated on Nippon Hill. Total Japanese losses in the Imphal battles were 54,879 according to official Japanese records. (*Imperial War Museum*)

11. Mule lines as troops await orders to advance on Mandalay, March 1945. (*Imperial War Museum*)

12. Indian casualties from 19 (Dagger) Division receiving first line treatment during the assault on Mandalay, March 1945. (*Imperial War Museum*)

13. A Japanese notice on the road between Maymyo and Mandalay in Burmese, Japanese and broken English.
(*Imperial War Museum*)

14. Japanese dead lying by their foxholes, Mandalay, 1945.
(*Imperial War Museum*)

15. "And so they were married": St Matthew's, Bayswater, 25 May, 1946.

16. The author in 1964 when 2 i/c of 13 Signal Regiment in Germany.

hostile tribesmen took advantage of our lax attitude in this respect.

I took to Paddy Roy as soon as I met him. He was a good bit older than me, a pre-war soldier who had been a sergeant in 1939 and who had been given an Emergency Commission early in the war. From the start, he took a paternal interest in me and I was to learn a great deal from him during the six months spent as his second-in-command. The Brigade Signal Section was made up of both British and Indian soldiers, the latter being Madrassis. As a generality, the Madrassi soldier was of higher intelligence than most other Indian soldiers but was less robust and aggressive. He was very dark-skinned and as different from the men from Northern India as a Southern Italian is from a Scandinavian; yet, in addition to a good sense of humour, he had great determination and staying power under good leadership. I found that our wireless operators and technicians were excellent tradesmen. The transport of the Section was a mixture of somewhat old motor vehicles (there were no jeeps in the Section as yet) and the indispensable mule. I was soon to discover that, once off the few tarmac roads on the Frontier, the mule was every bit as important to us as he was in the Burmese jungle.

Under Paddy Roy's guidance, and from my own involvement very soon after my arrival, it became apparent to me that the big military event of every week for the Brigade was the "Road Open Day" (ROD). Because this operation was repeated weekly throughout my six months with Bannu Brigade, it is worthy of explanation and description. The object of the exercise was to enable a convoy of vehicles, carrying resupply of rations, water and ammunition, to get through safely to the various forts each week without ambush or molestation by hostile tribesmen. The method was relatively simple and had been well tried for many years. A battalion of the Brigade would leave Bannu on one of the roads leading to the nearby mountains. Platoons from the two leading companies of the battalion would be sent up the hillsides on either side of the road to form pickets in sangars, sited at suitable locations in the heights overlooking the road. The remaining two rifle companies of this battalion would move up this protected section of the road with battalion headquarters

69

and with support elements of HQ Company. These two rifle companies in the second wave would picket the hills on either side of the road further on and then the second battalion of the Brigade would pass through on the road, with Tactical Brigade Headquarters and the main operational elements of the Signal Section in company. This second battalion would continue the same process of picketing the road ahead. A convoy of heavy supply vehicles would by now be inside the protected area of the road, close to but behind Tac Bde HQ. The third battalion of the Brigade would now leave Bannu and pass through the other two battalions and picket the hills on either side of the road still further on. The first battalion would then come down off the first picket locations, form a rearguard and move through the deployed Brigade until they were once again in the lead up the road. Tac Bde HQ, the Signal Section (less detachments with the three Bn HQs) and the supply convoy would move slowly up the road protected by the pickets, as each battalion in turn took the lead, protected the centre or formed the rearguard. In this way the whole Brigade moved up the road through the mountains and eventually reached a point where the supply convoy could deliver supplies to the fort concerned. The return journey to Bannu with the empty supply vehicles (and any personnel transfers or other cargo to be withdrawn from the fort) would be accomplished in exactly the same manner but, of course, in the opposite direction. Sometimes the distance to the fort to be supplied was too far for this manoeuvre to be achieved in one day or by one brigade. In this case it was usual for the garrison of the larger and more distant forts to come to meet us in a similar manner, picketing the hills as they came, and the convoy would be handed over midway between Bannu and the fort concerned. We would then return to Bannu in the same manner, sometimes bringing back with us an empty convoy of vehicles from a previous ROD.

These deployments required careful coordination throughout, and good communications between all elements involved were vital. Sometimes we took with us a battery of mountain artillery, carried on mules, to give supporting fire in case of attack by tribesmen. Good wireless communications from Tac Bde HQ to Bn HQs and the artillery battery were essential and we also had to provide a wireless link to Bannu, to the fort we were approaching and to the force coming down the road to meet us on those occasions when a joint ROD was necessary. We were still equipped with FS 6 sets and the equipment of each detachment was carried on three mules. The first carried the transmitter/receiver on one side of the saddle, batteries on the other side and the vibrator unit as a top load (it was possible to operate the set without unloading from the mule and operation on the move was not uncommon). The second mule carried a 350 watt charging engine (chore horse) as top load, with petrol and spare batteries as side loads. The third mule carried aerial gear, spares, petrol and some kit for the detachment. Each detachment would have a naik (corporal) or lance-naik wireless operator as detachment commander, two signalmen wireless operators and three signalmen mule leaders (known as Signals Assistants Animal Transport or "SAATs"). Thus a junior NCO and five men formed a detachment. Communications with pickets on the hills were a battalion signals responsibility and were frequently by visual signalling. Heliographs, lamps daylight signalling and single flag morse signalling were all used.

From time to time we would have a brush with hostile tribesmen, who seemed to enjoy sniping at the pickets and at troops moving on the road. Sometimes these encounters became more serious and a small battle would develop, requiring use of reserves or artillery and controlled by Tac Bde HQ. However, the tribesmen would usually disappear as soon as we began to vary the pattern and display the possibility of offensive or punitive action. On the average ROD pursuit of hostile tribesmen was never ordered. It would have been useless folly and very dangerous for the troops sent in pursuit. We usually had excellent intelligence information concerning expected activities by hostile tribesmen from such organizations as the Tochi Scouts. If at any time matters seemed to be getting out of hand and a particular tribe or collection of tribes became too troublesome, the remedy was first to levy a fine on the villages concerned. If this did not produce results, a punitive expedition would be mounted, but, although there were contingency plans for such an eventuality, this was a very rare occurrence and did not prove to be necessary during my time in Waziristan.

Some of the larger forts were maintained at brigade strength. As I recall, there was a Razmak Brigade and a Gardai Brigade, while other forts had a garrison of one battalion or more. There were occasions when the ROD for a particular week took a slightly different pattern. In order to open a particular road for several hours, so that traffic could pass from one fort to another (or between Bannu and a particular fort) in both directions and fully protected by pickets, two brigades or more would be deployed to cover the whole length of that road for several hours. After this, traffic would be stopped and the deployed units and formations would withdraw in the manner already described.

These routines were repeated in some form week in and week out. For the infantry soldiers, picketing the hills meant repeatedly doubling up hills to reach and establish their defensive positions, sometimes under sniper fire. This was hot, dusty work and, unless they were extremely fit, they would be breathless and unable to fire their weapons with accuracy when reaching the hill position. Later they would have to double down to the road again, move up the road and go through the whole process again, and again, and again. As a result, a high state of physical fitness was essential, for it was an exhausting drill. The fresh clean air of the mountains was a help and our situation was ideal for becoming and keeping very fit.

After the first few weeks in Bannu, by which time I had been taught the form on RODs, I did not have to go out every time the Brigade opened the road in this way. Paddy Roy would go with Tac Bde HQ one week and I the next. On occasions only one battalion of the Brigade would be involved and Tac Bde HQ and the Signal Section were not required, except for the wireless detachment with the Bn HQ concerned; but such occasions were very rare. For the rest of a working week we would be involved in the normal routine of Army Life in barracks – weapon training, trade training, PT, inspections and parades, administration, dealing with breaches of discipline and so on. Attention to our mules and motor transport was a high priority and we had a busy time in normal working hours, keeping all our equipment up to scratch and our soldiers on their toes. They were a happy lot, but we had the usual compassionate cases and personal problems of any unit to deal with, which was all good training for me in the business of man-management.

In off-duty moments I began to have a very active social life in Bannu. I developed a routine of playing tennis after work, followed by a long swim in the pool at the Officers' Club. My tennis was improved greatly with the help of the Club ball boys, young Wazirs who were employed to work on the hard courts collecting tennis balls, but who, over the years, developed great skill at returning, hard, fast and with great accuracy, any ball you fired at them.

I soon had a girlfriend, who was a nurse at the hospital, although my heart was still very much in Kashmir. Her name was Noreen Rosner and she was blonde, beautiful and about my age. I was to discover later that her father was a German living in Burma and that her mother was Anglo-Burmese. She and her mother had escaped from Burma into India at the time of the 1942 retreat (when I was in Bangalore as an infantry officer-cadet) but her father had stayed on in Burma. I presume that, as a German, he had felt that he would have no trouble from the Japanese occupation forces, as the German Nazis and the Japanese were allies as members of the so-called "Berlin–Rome–Tokyo Axis", against which we and the civilized world were fighting for survival. I did not know this when I first met Noreen but she told me her background later, when we knew one another better. On arrival in India in 1942 (as a refugee), she had left her mother in a small flat in Calcutta. I was later to call on her and meet her for the first and only time on my way through Calcutta to return to the fighting in Burma. Noreen had joined the Indian Nursing Service and, after training had been posted to the Military Hospital in Bannu. She was a delightful person, but when, later, I discovered that her father was a German and was still in Burma, I allowed our friendship to cool, although we kept in touch for the rest of my time in the Far East. I feared possible security complications. Perhaps I was overcautious and unfair in this respect, but, though I was young, I was already aware of the risks involved and decided that discretion was the better part of valour.

There were dances and parties at the Officers' Club and

generally life was very relaxed and pleasant during off-duty hours. It became easy to forget that there was a particularly bloody war being waged with the Japanese on the eastern borders of India. I shared a bungalow with Paddy Roy. This accommodation was provided by the Garrison as Officers' Bachelor Quarters and included two bedrooms, a large living room which we shared, two bathrooms (which were next to our bedrooms but which were very fundamental, with tin baths filled with warm water by our bearers, using used ghi tins!) and with the kitchen and our bearers' quarters in the compound but separate from the main building. Both Paddy Roy and I felt free to entertain our girlfriends in our bungalow and we also had a number of very good parties there, until, one day, we both received a formal letter from Garrison Headquarters, concise and to the point, which informed us that we were occupying Army *bachelor* quarters and were contravening Garrison Order Number so-and-so by enter-taining ladies therein! It was necessary, therefore, for us both to be very much more careful from then on, and this we were! We felt sure that somebody, who was less fortunate than ourselves with his social life, had reported our activities to Garrison Headquarters, but we never did find out who the culprit was, although we had our suspicions.

As the months went by, I began to learn more and more about the problems, pitfalls and solutions of administration in a typi-cal Indian Army unit. This was another completely new experience for me and it had its amusing as well as its serious and annoying moments. Because I had been with a Gurkha Column for most of Operation "LONGCLOTH" and, know-ing no Gurkhali, had got by with English, I had not been called upon to speak much of the Urdu I had been taught as an Officer Cadet. Now my Urdu was essential if I was to be understood by my Indian soldiers in Bannu. Although Madrassi, they could all speak Urdu and some had a smattering of English as well. Thus force of circumstances made me more and more fluent in that part of the Urdu language in general use by Indian soldiers.

After about three months in Bannu a chance remark in Urdu, which I overheard, put me on the trail of a little mild corrup-tion occurring within the Section. The Orderly Room Havildar

(Sergeant), with a somewhat sarcastic smirk on his face, was asking one of our mule leaders (SAATs): "*Apka darja kya hai?*" ("What is your rank?"). In the first place, he knew very well that the man concerned was a signalman and the use of "*apka*" (a sign of deference to a superior) instead of "*tumhara*" for "your", made me prick up my ears. I knew that the SAAT concerned, although not particularly bright, was one of the best of the signalmen mule leaders. I also knew that Paddy Roy and I had agreed that he should be promoted to Lance Naik. We had warned the Orderly Room Havildar to publish this promotion in Section Orders the following week but on no account was he to inform the SAAT beforehand. As a consequence, I remained concealed and did a bit more eavesdropping. It transpired that the Orderly Room Havildar was asking the SAAT if he would like to be promoted to Lance Naik and earn more pay. When the SAAT replied in the affirmative, the Havildar said he could fix it and named the price in rupees that he required for this favour. Needless to say, I then discussed this matter with Paddy Roy. We investigated a number of recent promotions to junior NCO and found that the Orderly Room Havildar had been running this racket for some time, choosing his victims from the less intelligent of his comrades. The upshot of all this was that the Havildar was reduced to the ranks and posted, and a new and more trustworthy Orderly Room Havildar was appointed to replace him.

Another aspect of behaviour of many Indian soldiers, to which I was introduced for the first time in Bannu, was their use of the professional writer of "letters of application", usually to be found in the local bazaar. These characters, who professed a knowledge not only of written English but also the correct format of a military application, would write a letter as from a soldier and covering a wide variety of different matters according to the wishes of his customer, the soldier. A modest fee for each letter would be charged and the soldier would then present the written application to his officer for consideration. The most common type of letter was an application for leave of absence on compassionate grounds. There was one particular professional letter writer who operated in the bazaar at Bannu whose letters were so hilarious that we looked forward to receiving and reading them as a guarantee of a good laugh. The usual reason given for an urgent need for the soldier to be granted leave was the serious illness of a close relative (or of many close relatives!). The number of times we were told, in a succession of applications, that a particular soldier's grand-mother, cousin, sister, etc, etc was or were about to die was legion. I remember one particular letter which, after the usual heart-rending reasons for requesting leave, ended with the sen-tence: "If your honour does not see fit to grant this leave, may I please be excused PT?" We took more seriously the presen-tation of a telegram, sent from Madrás or some village or town in Southern India, the text of which usually took the form "Father (or some other relative) soon die. Reach." If one of our soldiers came to see Paddy Roy or myself and showed us a telegram of this type, we would telegram the local police at the place of origin for confirmation, on receipt of which the soldier would be sent on leave immediately. The term "reach" was often used and meant "come at once"!

One month followed another with a similar routine and these were happy times for me. The war seemed to be miles away in another world and we soldiered on in Waziristan in much the same way as our predecessors had done for generations past. We watched the news, particularly of the war in Burma where, for the moment, it seemed that there was something of a stalemate. Anxiety about a possible invasion of India though Afghanistan by the Nazis (at one time, when the Russians were in full retreat, considered to be a real possibility) had now receded, with the Russians pushing the Germans back towards the west. Once again we felt that we were in a backwater, with only the Frontier tribesmen to worry about. In November 1943 I was sent to the Command School at Rawalpindi to attend an Administration Course. It was quite useful but much of the instruction covered matters that I had been learning by experience and under the guidance of Paddy Roy in Bannu. Much was also a reiteration of the instruction we had been given on Indian Army adminis-tration at the OCTU. The course finished on 15 December 1943 and it occurred to me that, as I was in Rawalpindi, I might try to take two weeks' leave and go up to Kashmir for Christmas. The first thing to do was to find out whether M could have me to stay with her. I managed to get through to Srinagar by telephone. It was a terrible line but eventually I managed to talk to her. She told me she would love to have me for Christmas but the road through the mountains to Srinagar was completely blocked by snow and was likely to remain so for the next few weeks. Sadly, I had to abandon plans for yet another leave in Kashmir that year and returned disappointed to Bannu. I was to see M and Srinagar again in August 1944, after the Imphal/Kohima battles had been won.

When I arrived back in Bannu Garrison I found waiting for me a summons to appear before a Medical Board at the Military Hospital. I reported for this soon after my return and was pronounced completely fit – category A1. The result of the Medical Board must have been reported by signal to GHQ, New Delhi, as, just before Christmas, my posting back to the war in Burma arrived. I was required to travel via Calcutta to Comilla and report to HQ 14th Army for further instructions. In due course I received a Movement Order from HQ Waziristan District which required me to move by train early in the New Year to Rawalpindi and thence to Calcutta, where I would be given further instructions for the onward move to Comilla. All this had happened almost two months sooner than I had expected.

Christmas 1943 in Bannu was a happy yet sad occasion for me. I had made many good friends in the months I had spent there and was sorry to be leaving the place. Yet I felt that a return to the war in Burma would be a return to reality and would give me a chance to prove my worth after what I regarded as the fiasco of "LONGCLOTH" during which I had not once seen the Japanese enemy (although they had been nearby often enough) and had marched myself almost to death across Burma to Yunnan without seeming to have done anything positive enough to justify the agony and hardship of it all. In Bannu we had a spate of Christmas parties and then a wonderful farewell party was given to see me on my way. I do not believe that they were celebrating my departure in the spirit of "Thank God he is going". I just think they were sad to say goodbye to me and wanted to wish me luck in my somewhat uncertain future. In any event it was a damn good party which I still remember with gratitude after all these years; and so, on

5 January 1944, I left Bannu, Noreen Rosner and all my friends and headed back to the real war.

When I reached Rawalpindi from Mari-Indus, the Movements people there examined my movement order and got me onto a train to Lahore. I was travelling in the right direction but I had hoped to go all the way through to Calcutta without having to change trains. At least I had a comfortable compartment. The train was not an express but the journey to Lahore was soon accomplished. I remember we stopped for some time at Jhelum, because I got off the train there and had a meal in the station restaurant while the train waited for us, the "sahibs"! At Lahore I again reported to Movements at the station and they put me on a train to Delhi, which travelled through the night by way of Amritsar, Ludhiana and Ambala the home of the 15th Punjab Regiment. Once again I contacted Movements, this time on the main railway station at Delhi, and at last they found me a comfortable sleeping compartment on a train which would take me through to Calcutta without the need to change trains again. This was by far the longest stretch of the whole journey, taking us through Agra, Cawnpore, then along the valley of the River Ganges to Allahabad and Benares, and then onwards across Bihar to Calcutta. It had taken me over two days and nights to get this far and by this time I felt tired, dirty and somewhat fed up with trains.

I again reported to Movements at Calcutta railway station and they organized transport to take me and my small amount of luggage to the Grand Hotel, a somewhat grand name for a hotel in Calcutta which had been taken over by the Army authorities as an Officers' transit accommodation. At one time it had been quite a nice hotel, but since Calcutta had become "the roaring town behind the Front" (as it was sometimes described) it was packed to overflowing with British officers, from both the Indian and British Armies, who were passing through Calcutta. We were sleeping five or six to a bedroom designed for one, or at most two. Food and drink were quite adequate but there was always a long wait to be served. The Grand Hotel had been the second best hotel in Calcutta. Typically, it had been requisitioned for *British* officers in transit. The best hotel in Calcutta, the Great Eastern, had been taken over as a transit accommodation for US Officers (mainly US Air Force). Their numbers were very small compared with ours but they seemed to have been given the best of the bargain, which caused considerable resentment. After all, the Burma war was very much more a British than an American affair. The US Air Force, with the RAF, gave us wonderful air support in Burma, particularly in the business of dropping supplies to us from the air, but the fighting by ground forces was predominantly our province. Nevertheless I owed the Americans a great personal debt, for they had taken me from China, flown me back to India from Yunnan after "LONGCLOTH", and so had probably saved my life.

There was a vast entrance foyer to the Grand Hotel. This was filled with small tables and chairs and was usually packed to capacity, or more, with officers drinking and talking to while away the days of waiting for their next move, either on posting, on leave or back to the fighting. The noise in this foyer was deafening and it usually took a long time to get across it to the lifts, stairs or dining room. This was because, as one progressed, an arm would be raised to grab yours and a voice would say, "Good Lord, I haven't seen you since . . . ! Glad to know you are still alive and kicking. Sit down and have a drink," or some other words in similar vein. This hazard was repeated again and again when trying to cross the foyer to one's room or to the dining room. There were occasions when the whole place burst into song (sometimes the songs were a bit near the bone). I remember one, probably of American origin, which I had not heard before but which I was to hear quite often in the foyer of the Grand Hotel. This was the ditty starting:

"Cocaine Joe and Morphine Sue
Were strolling down the Avenue,"

with the chorus:

"Have a little sniff, have a sniff on me
Have a little sniff on me."

But the word "sniff" was said, as a sniff, with the back of everyone's hand brought up to their nose each time the "sniff"

79

occurred in the chorus! There were many verses, but I cannot remember them all. What I do remember vividly, however, is the spectacle of hundreds of young men singing together in unison and making a rythmical but deafening noise, while hundreds of hands were lifted to hundreds of noses in time with the appropriate words of the chorus.

This sort of song was just an outpouring of blessed relief from the horror of war and an expression of the joy of still being alive. There was no harm in it and, with regard to the stupid song I have mentioned, I did not once hear of a case of drug addiction among British soldiers in those days. In fact it was unheard of, although some Indian soldiers were opium addicts and it was possible, and indeed authorized, for an issue of opium to be made by the quartermaster on a regular basis to those Indian soldiers who were officially registered as opium addicts.

To reach Comilla, Movements had to arrange a journey which would involve train, ferry, train, another ferry and then completion of the journey by road. There were quite a few of us who were waiting for this journey to be arranged. Meanwhile we languished in the Grand Hotel or explored Calcutta. At last a list was posted on the noticeboard in the foyer of the hotel, with the names of those officers, including myself, who were to start the journey to Comilla the following morning. We were taken in Army transport to the railway station and the tedious journey began. I remember a night ferry crossing, along and across a wide river which must have been the Ganges near its mouth, where it entered the Bay of Bengal. This was followed by a long and uncomfortable journey by road. Eventually we arrived at a large reinforcement and transit camp on the outskirts of Comilla, in what is now Bangladesh. I waited in this camp for two or three weeks and was kitted out again for the jungle. All the clothes that I would take with me into Burma, including underclothes and handkerchiefs, were dyed green. I had suffered this once before, at Meerut before I joined 77 Brigade for Operation "LONGCLOTH", but I had completely re-kitted myself with khaki drill, white underclothes and other "normal" items of clothing for my time in Waziristan. Now all the unwanted new clothing and equipment was packed

80

away in my metal uniform trunk and sent to an organization located near Comilla and called "20 Div Dump" (this was after I had been told I was to join 20th Indian Division), there to disappear without trace. I was never to see these personal possessions again. Two suits of jungle green denim battle dress were issued, to join all my other personal gear which I had preserved from my days with Special Force in anticipation of my return to the war in Burma. A new type of jungle hat also came my way – not the Australian-type wide-brimmed jungle hat but a lightweight green hat with a narrower brim, which I believe was made of synthetic cloth with a fibreglass thread incorporated. It was very hard-wearing and helped to keep the head cool. Perhaps the three most important items of personal kit that I had been careful to preserve for my return to Burma were my boots, my kukri and my framed big pack. The latter was an absolute boon, enabling me to march with a heavy load on my back, yet, with the frame, providing that cooling circulation of air between pack and back which made such a difference on long-distance marches over difficult country.

After waiting impatiently in the transit camp, I was called one day to Chief Signal Officer (CSO) Branch at HQ 14th Army and told that I had been selected for posting to 20th Indian Division as the second-in-command of 80 Brigade Signal Section. I was told that the Division was based on Tamu, in the Kabaw Valley east of Imphal, and that 80 Brigade was at that time deployed to cover the country to the north-east of Tamu up to the River Chindwin. Almost exactly a year before this, in February 1943, I had marched through this area with Nos 1 and 2 columns of 77 Brigade and had crossed the Chindwin at the beginning of that long slog into enemy territory which, for me, was the main memory of "LONGCLOTH". As a consequence, I knew a little about my new destination. I was told by CSO Branch that I would be flown in to Imphal in the near future and would be taken from the airstrip to join 80 Brigade under arrangements to be made by 20 Divisional Signals. No doubt I would be met on landing by transport to take me down to Tamu and beyond. I returned to the Comilla transit camp and waited for several more days until, at last, I was ordered to the airfield and boarded a DC3 Dakota aircraft with others who were also reinforcements being flown in to the Imphal area. We landed at the airstrip at Palel, a jeep from 20 Divisional Signals was there to meet me and we drove up to and over Shenam Ridge, through an area I was to get to know only too well in the near future, and down into the Kabaw Valley, through Moreh to Divisional HQ near Tamu.

By now it was mid-February 1944 and within four weeks the most important battle of the Burma campaign, and one of the most important battles of the Second World War, would be upon us.

Chapter 5

THE SIEGE OF IMPHAL
MARCH TO JULY 1944

In February 1944 20 Indian Division formed part of 4 Corps and was facing the Japanese in the area of Tamu, on the banks of the River Chindwin to the east of the Imphal plain in the border state of Manipur.

The Ides of March in the year 1944 saw the commencement of an onslaught by the Japanese upon India which very nearly ended in complete success. Few people in India or the rest of the world realize, even now, how great was the threat to our stronghold in the Far East during those dark days following 15 March 1944. The first move in the game was a strong feint attack upon our forces in the Arakan, on the coast, with the obvious hope of diverting reserves and reinforcements to that sector. Although this move did not prove to be a great success for the Japanese, it nevertheless diverted attention to the southern sector and enabled the enemy to hold the initiative for his main onslaught on the central sector, with the Imphal Plain as his primary and the Assam railway as his secondary objectives.

Accordingly on 15 March 1944 three Japanese divisions (31, 15, and 33 Divisions) – a total of more than 50,000 men – went on to the offensive after crossing the River Chindwin. They were divided into four main attacking groups. One (31 Division – SATO) headed via Tamanthi and Homalin for Kohima, there to cut the road and push on to the railway at Dimapur. The second group, made up in part from 31 Division and commanded by Miyazaki but consisting mainly of 15 Division (Yamauchi), marched via Homalin and Tonhe to Ukhrul and onwards towards the Imphal Plain and the main Dimapur road. The third group Yamamoto Force, which was made up of part of 15 Division and part of 33 Division, marched past Tamu, intending to encircle our forces there and, having dealt with them, was to move through the hills to Imphal. The fourth group (33 Division – Yanagida) cut off our forces to the south in Tiddim and, having dealt with them, was to advance northwards to the Imphal Plain.

At the start of this offensive the British forces which withstood the shock consisted of three infantry divisions and one Parachute Brigade (50 Indian Parachute Brigade). The latter had been sent to Imphal in a ground role "to gain practical battle experience". Needless to say, they gained plenty.

17 Indian Division was holding Tiddim, in the south; 20 Indian Division was in the Tamu area in the Kabaw Valley, extended to the banks of the River Chindwin, and 23 Indian Division was resting on the Imphal Plain, having been down on the banks of the Chindwin almost continuously since the 1942 retreat from Burma. The Parachute Brigade was concentrated in the Ukhrul area, which was then thought to be a quiet sector by reason of the impossible country over which the enemy would have to advance to reach Ukhrul. Such was the original force which made up 4 Indian Corps.

At Kohima the garrison, commanded by Colonel Hugh Richards, consisted of a battalion of the Assam Rifles and a few odds and ends in Leave and Reinforcements Camps, joined by 500 men of the 4th Battalion of the Royal West Kents, under the command of Lt Col Danny Laverty, just before the place was surrounded. This totally inadequate force performed a miracle of defence against a complete division of Japanese by holding on to Kohima for 22 days before relief came. In the initial stages of the offensive this heroic body of men stood alone between a Japanese division and the vital Assam railway – and India – and they held the onslaught until reinforcements arrived.

This, then, was the force which withstood the first blows. Later fresh troops arrived to relieve the situation. 2 British Division relieved Kohima and stopped any further Japanese threat to the railway, eventually re-opening the road to beleaguered Imphal, together with two Brigades of the veteran 5 Indian Division. 4 Indian Corps was soon surrounded holding the Imphal Plain and was cut off from the outside world except by air. The siege of Imphal – and of 4 Corps – had begun. 17 Division fought its way back from Tiddim, with the help of elements of 23 Division, and stood on the Southern extremities of the Imphal Plain. 20 Division fought its way back from Tamu and the Kabaw Valley, over the mountains to Shenam Ridge – the highest point between Imphal and Tamu – and there turned and faced the enemy. The Indian Parachute Brigade at Sangshak, near Ukhrul, had been badly cut up by the overwhelming force of the second group (part 15 and part 31 Japanese Divisions) and the survivors were forced to withdraw to the northern edge of the Imphal Plain where, with elements of 23 Indian Division, they held on and restored the situation. Meanwhile a Brigade of 5 Indian Division was flown in to the Imphal garrison and held the Imphal end of the main Dimapur Road. The Silchar track from Imphal westwards to Assam was also cut and 4 Corps remained surrounded and besieged for the next four months, supplied entirely by air and under orders to hold the Imphal Plain at all costs.

I had no inkling of any of this when I joined 80 Brigade and arrived at the Headquarters, which was located under a tree in a clearing in the jungle-clad hills to the south-west of Thaungdut, a village on the banks of the River Chindwin. I was welcomed by my new OC, Captain "Johnnie" Brown, who introduced me to our Brigadier, Sam Greaves, and to other members of the Headquarters. We did not know it then but we were on the eve of the worst period of fighting that I was to experience during the whole Burma campaign. I did not expect that within weeks of my arrival Johnnie Brown was to be killed in action and I would find myself in temporary command of the Brigade Signal Section until Captain "Daddy" Major, a splendid Parsee officer from Indian Signals, would arrive as his replacement. Nor could I visualize the horrors I was to experience during the four critical months from mid-March until mid-July 1944 that the battles of Imphal and Kohima lasted.

When at last the siege of Imphal was lifted and the battle won, the majority of us in the Brigade who had survived were sent back to India at some time during the following three months for two weeks' leave, measured to and from crossing the River Brahmaputra. I took my leave in late August and went straight to Kashmir. I found myself longing to be with M again and to feel once more the peace and security of her lovely home by Dal Lake in Srinagar. I arrived there a somewhat shattered man. Poor M only seemed to meet me when I was down but she welcomed me with open arms and I will never forget her kindness and understanding. During this leave I felt compelled to write in detail about my personal experiences of this prolonged battle for Imphal, a battle which was as important to our success in the Burma Campaign as Alamein was to the campaign in North Africa. With little alteration I have preserved this account over the years and, since it was written so soon after the events described, I have included it here virtually word for word:-

The Battle For Imphal – Shenam and the Iril Valley

It was February 1944 when I came again to the banks of the Chindwin, almost exactly a year after my first sight of the river. This time the circumstances were different. I was not just passing through, to cross secretly to the eastern bank and march off through the jungles of Japanese-held Burma, to come out

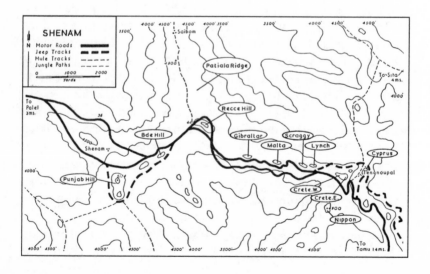

after many exhausting, eventful and often frightening weeks, through to China and an airlift back to India and hospital. No longer the expectation of prolonged marching and fighting deep in enemy territory; this time I was with a Brigade of a standard Indian Division. The task was to sit on the western bank, patrol southwards into the dense and disease-filled jungle of the Kabaw Valley and northwards towards Homalin; to watch across the river for signs of enemy activity. The Division was based on Tamu.

80 Brigade of 20th Indian Division was commanded by Brigadier Sam Greaves. The three battalions were 1st Devon, 9th/12th Frontier Force Rifles, and 3rd/1st Gurkha Rifles. I was second-in-command of the Brigade Signal Section and, at the time of my joining the Brigade, the Officer Commanding was Captain "Johnnie" Brown, Royal Signals. The section was a mixed unit of British and Indian soldiers and was approximately 100 strong. We had mules as primary transport, with a few jeeps for use when tracks were wide enough to allow this. At this time we were equipped with an Australian-manufactured pack wireless equipment (the FS6 set) which made a neat saddle load for a mule (transmitter/receiver on one side, battery on the other side and vibrator unit as a top load on the saddle). Unfortunately the performance of these equipments was very poor, giving a maximum range of 2 to 3 miles on voice transmissions, although we had managed to get by in the Chindits on Operation "LONG-CLOTH" with the same FS6 Sets, using handspeed Morse HF Skywave over distances in excess of 300 miles. We were expecting to refit with the then new WS22 when I arrived at Tamu to join the Brigade. As a consequence of the poor performance of the FS6, I found that the Section had come to rely upon field cable and despatch rider services in the difficult wireless country in the valley of the River Chindwin. With great good fortune our new WS22 arrived by the end of February and we were just learning to get the best out of these new equipments when the Japanese offensive began in early March 1944.

At first the enemy attacks seemed to be somewhat disjointed and concentrated mainly on our lines of communication back to the Imphal Plain. The Tamu track, our only lifeline for resupply by vehicle, was cut and we started to depend more and more on

87

resupply by parachute from the air. As part of a pre-arranged plan, the Division began a withdrawal through the Naga Hills towards Palel, with 80 Brigade forming the rearguard. For the next two weeks we were obliged to fight our way back along the Tamu track, clearing numerous blocks set up by the Japanese who had cut the track in many places to our rear. This was a difficult period for us all, as we were constantly on the move and having to fight our way out of a dangerous situation. The Brigade eventually reached the highest point in the Naga Hills between Tamu and the Imphal Plain at a ridge collectively known as Shenam, where we took over from 100 Brigade, a "sister" Brigade in 20 Division, which had withdrawn from the Kabaw Valley ahead of us and was now required elsewhere in the defence of the Imphal Plain. Here at Shenam we were ordered to dig in, to hold and to consolidate our positions, for no further withdrawal could be countenanced. The last Japanese block before reaching Shenam was at Tengnoupal Peak, which directly overshadowed the track along which we had to pass. The area was very mountainous. The sheer sides of features made defence easier once possession had been established and Tengnoupal (later to become known as "Nippon") Peak was to be a thorn in our sides for the next two months. The immediate problem was to get the Brigade past this feature and on to our planned positions at Shenam with a minimum of losses to our artillery, transport and essentials. This was achieved by the most desperate fighting by 3/1st Gurkha Rifles, who put in attack after attack on the Japanese who were well dug into the summit of Tengnoupal, while the remainder of the Brigade slipped past to take up and consolidate their positions on the remaining hill features which constituted the Shenam Ridge. In spite of their efforts, the 3/1st Gurkha Rifles did not succeed in taking Tengnoupal and we were soon to find, to our extreme discomfort, that much of the Shenam area was dominated by this hilltop. However, the Brigade arrived intact at their selected defensive positions on the various hilltops of Shenam and, although the fighting withdrawal had resulted in a number of casualties, we were well pleased with ourselves to have reached the area from which there could be no further retreat. By this time the whole Imphal Plain had been surrounded and we were besieged. The only contact with the outside world was by air and we were to remain in this unenviable position for the next three months. To the south, 17th Division had withdrawn on the southern edge of the Plain from Tiddim and they too had to undertake a fighting withdrawal.

As an introduction to the hard facts of war, I had been in action during the first six months of 1943, as a member of Wingate's Long Range Penetration Operation, but somehow, in spite of the hardships, fear and anxieties of those times, it had all been an adventure. In those days we had known of unspeakable brutalities by the Japanese to those of our comrades who had been unfortunate enough to fall into their hands but we had avoided contact with the Japanese whenever possible and it had been a hit-and-run affair. Shenam was different. This was my first encounter with the full futile horror of war. We were involved in the dogged defence of hilltops in the mountainous country of the Naga Hills, against the determined and seemingly endless series of frontal attacks on these positions by a very brave and brutal enemy. We lived for weeks in holes in the ground with a mounting pile of dead Japanese bodies outside our wire, as more and more died in their attacks on our positions. More often than not we were able to evacuate our own injured and bury our dead, but it was common for this not to be immediately possible because we were often surrounded on our hilltops for long periods. The Japanese dead stayed where they lay, a carpet of mushroom-like camouflaged steel helmets which thickened in texture as each night passed and the number of dead outside our wire increased. The whole area became a shambles reminiscent of conditions on the Western Front in the First World War. The jungle-clad hillsides were soon cleared of vegetation by the shelling; the constant fire fights, attacks and counter-attacks left the whole area carpeted with dead bodies in inaccessible places. Here they rotted as the battle continued for weeks and Shenam Ridge soon began to smell with that sweet, sickly, horrifying aroma of death. We all became filthy and very tired. Sleep could only be intermittent and our beds were the foxholes and ground where we fought. Fortunately the monsoons had not yet started and it was fairly dry for the first six weeks of the battle. We were never sure that we could hold our ground but realized that we must do so, as the whole of the Imphal Plain was surrounded and if we gave way there would be no escape. This was a period that seemed endless. It was a frightening and horrifying time, yet an extraordinary spirit developed among the British, Indian and Gurkha soldiers involved. No quarter was asked or given and a dogged exhausted determination grew, to hold our positions at all costs. In truth, both sides fought themselves almost to a standstill. Often the Japanese succeeded in breaking in to parts of our positions, only to be eliminated by counter-attacks to restore the full defensive layout. We came to believe that either we ourselves must be killed or that it would never end.

Maintaining communications between Brigade Headquarters and each hill position in these conditions was a hazardous business. On the face of it, the requirement was straightforward. The normal facilities of a Forward Command Net linking Brigade Headquarters with Battalion Headquarters by wireless had to be augmented by additional wireless stations on the same net providing communications between Brigade and each hilltop position. As there were six all-round defensive positions of importance on the Shenam Ridge, it can be understood that Battalions were divided among these positions, with the result that companies were often separated from their own Battalion Headquarters by territory which was frequently in the hands of the enemy. In addition to the Forward Command Net, the normal rear links to Headquarters 20 Division were essential to our survival, as our requirements for re-supply were passed back by this means.

To provide an essential back-up for the Forward Command Net it was vital that we linked all hilltop positions with each other by field cable. Our third means was by message carrying, which was hazardous at the best of times and became more and more difficult as the battle progressed. In time of extreme emergency, when all other means had failed, we even resorted to the use of visual communications by "Lamps Daylight Signalling" in order to get vital messages through.

Each of these means of communication proved to be vulnerable to the conditions of the battle. In the early stages enemy artillery fire was restricted to their best endeavours using pack howitzers; later they brought up field artillery and medium artillery and we did the same. The WS22 HF wireless transceiver with which we were equipped was excellent in its way but did not give twenty-four-hour service because of atmospheric conditions. Detachments were "taken out" from time to time by shellfire and aerials were frequently destroyed. Battery charging was a constant trouble in hilltop positions and, to add to our difficulties, the detachments, which consisted of a Corporal or a Naik and two operators, often had to leave the wireless weapon pit to join in desperate attempts to repel Japanese who had broken into the perimeter. The field cable routes were also highly vulnerable and developed constant faults, either because the cable was cut by shelling or because of deliberate enemy action. We used D3 single earth return and the thicker D8 twisted and, as far as possible, we laid alternative routes. We soon discovered to our cost that the enemy would deliberately put a fault on these routes by cutting the cable and would then wait in ambush at the point of fault and engage the line party as they arrived to carry out their repairs. As a consequence we soon took to providing an escort for each line party and frequent fire fights would develop which became quite prolonged engagements and cost us a number of men. Our OC Brigade Signals, Captain Brown, was killed within two weeks of arriving at Shenam while working with a line party which was ambushed and, shortly after this, I myself had my very first experience of close-quarter hand-to-hand fighting during a similar encounter with the enemy. Message-carrying by SDS was also particularly hazardous both by night and by day as the despatch riders were popular targets for Japanese patrols and movement by day often called up immediate enemy shellfire. Even the small amount of visual signalling by lamp became highly dangerous as Japanese snipers (often tied to trees outside the hilltop positions) would "take out" either the light or the operator as soon as a signal was transmitted.

At this stage of the war the Japanese soldier still seemed to be without fear; he was brutal but very brave and gave the impression that he wanted to die in the fight. A saving grace was that his tactical approach to professional soldiering was unimaginative and his attacks were repetitious. The same routes and methods were used night after night and day after day so that we came to know what to expect. The assaults on most forward positions were both by night and day but those on the more rearward positions were mainly carried out at night. Almost invariably snipers were left behind after a night attack to continue harassment during the daylight hours.

Those of us who had fought the Japanese before were aware of their complete contempt for an enemy who allowed himself to be taken prisoner. At this stage in the war the number of Japanese soldiers held as prisoners in our hands was very small and these had almost invariably been captured because they were desperately wounded or unconscious at the time. It was commonplace for the Japanese to feign death when wounded and then to kill themselves and some of our men with a grenade rather than be captured. We came to realize that for them it was probably preferable to die in action than to fall into enemy hands.

Shortly after our arrival at Shenam, an incident occurred to a close friend which provided a clear illustration of the sort of treatment meted out to prisoners of war by the Japanese. A subaltern in the 9/12th FFR, Jeremy H..., who had been a fellow cadet with me at the Officer Training School at Bangalore in 1942, was taken while leading a patrol of ten "jawans" in the jungle some miles from our defensive positions. The patrol was ambushed and H... was stunned by a plastic grenade and left for dead. The survivors of his patrol scattered and returned to the battalion believing that their officer had been killed in the fight. H... was reported "missing believed killed" but crawled into Brigade positions a week later. He was in a dreadful condition and told us his story while awaiting evacuation to field hospital. When he recovered consciousness after being stunned by the grenade, he must have moved. He was only slightly wounded, being peppered on the right of his face and on his right shoulder with small pieces of plastic from the grenade casing. The Japanese soldiers nearby realized that he was alive. With boots and rifle butts, he was brought to his feet, his hands were tied behind his back and he was made to march through the jungle to a bivouac area some five miles away. There he was thrown to the ground, his lower clothing and boots removed and a fire was lit. He was severely beaten. They then applied burning embers from the fire to his genitals and the soles of his feet were burnt. The officer in charge of the Japanese patrol could speak a little English and, at intervals during this maltreatment, he was questioned about our dispositions at Shenam. Even if he had been completely willing to disclose this information, there was little that he could tell, as his knowledge of the Brigade situation at Shenam was limited to a very sketchy idea of his own company positions on first arrival. H . . . could not remember clearly the duration of this torture but it seemed to go on for a long time. Eventually the patrol moved off, dragging him with them at the end of a rope fixed around his neck, his wrists still tightly tied behind his back. He was dressed only in his shirt. Even if his boots had been returned to him, he could not have put them on. Walking was an agony but somehow he kept up with them. He had little alternative. After a time they were walking along a narrow path on a very steep hillside. He took his chance and threw himself from the path down the precipitous khud-side into the jungle below. He still had the rope around his neck and the other end of this must have been torn from the hands of his captor by the force of his fall. Evidently the distance was such that the Japanese did not try to follow him and must have believed him to be dead. He was knocked unconscious by the fall and, when he came to, he found himself in deep cover. By some miracle, no bones were broken and he started to crawl west-wards towards Shenam. His hands were still tied tightly behind his back and he could not free himself from these bonds; the rope tether was still around his neck with the loose end trailing behind him and he was still dressed only in his shirt. It took him four days and nights to reach Shenam and he was in a very bad way when he was found by a patrol of 3rd/1st Gurkha Rifles just outside the Brigade positions. Jeremy H . . . was evacuated to base hospital by air, the only way out of Imphal at that time. (Six months later he was back with his battalion for the advance across Burma and was killed in action. He was 22 years old when he died.)

By force of circumstances, our activities were not confined exclusively to the defence of the hill positions of Shenam. Major-General Yamamoto and his 33rd Japanese Division were determined to break through the Shenam defences and reach the Imphal Plain. When the main Japanese thrust came to a standstill and a battle of attrition developed, the enemy tried to infiltrate past our positions through the thick jungle and mountainous country on the flanks of the Palel-Tamu Road. To counter such moves, it was necessary to patrol in strength through this difficult country, between Shenam and Leitan to the north-east and between Shenam and Shuganu to the south-west. These patrols were arduous in the extreme, for the jungle was so thick and the hills and ridges so numerous and steep-sided that covering the ground was often found to be as much of a problem as dealing with the Japanese encountered in the course of these forays. Patrols were usually of platoon strength but, on occasions, an entire company with a small number of mules for essential loads would be away for two weeks or more on such an expedition. Communications with Brigade Headquarters or battalion could only be by wireless and "standby" detachments of the Brigade Signal Section were frequently used for this purpose. The WS22 with battery and charging engine (known as a "chore horse") with spare batteries were carried on two strong "artillery" mules and a third mule completed the transport of the detachment, carrying spares, aerial gear and additional equipment for the NCO, two operators and the three mule leaders.

As a direct result of this patrol activity, we came to know the Naga tribesmen who inhabited this mountainous country. Later, during the Iril Valley operation, we got to know them even better and often harboured in their villages. Field Marshal Sir William Slim, in his book *Defeat into Victory*, had this to say about them:

> "These were the gallant Nagas whose loyalty, even in the most depressing times of the invasion, had never faltered. Despite floggings, torture, execution, and the burning of their villages, they refused to aid the Japanese in any way or to betray our troops. Their active help to us was beyond value or praise . . . they guided our columns, collected information, ambushed enemy patrols, carried our supplies, and brought in our wounded under the heaviest fire – and then, being the gentlemen they were, often refused all payment. Many a British and Indian soldier owes his life to the naked, head-hunting Naga, and no soldier of the Fourteenth Army who met them will ever think of them but with admiration and affection."

The Nagas are hill tribesmen who live a deprived life in an appalling climate. They live in village communities, the villages usually sited on the tops of ridges and hill features, often 6,000 feet or more above sea level and, particularly in the monsoon period, more often than not in mist or cloud. The Nagas collect their water from streams in the valleys far below, where the extreme heat and humidity produces dense jungle and very unhealthy conditions. They have a remarkable ability to climb up the steep mountainside with heavy head-loads at great speed. The family is the whole village and male and female cohabit as they wish within that village. Children born of such unions become the responsibility of the village as a whole and are well cared for within the limits of the sparse and frugal existence of the tribe. The men are head-hunters and are tough adversaries, even though their most common weapon is a long metal spear and a dah (a broad bladed cutting knife with a square tip – we found the dah to be ideal for cutting a path through thick jungle). The houses in their villages were thatched wooden shelters, for the most part built on stilts so that the lowest floor was two or three feet above the ground. This was particularly necessary during the monsoons, to keep the inhabitants as dry as possible during periods of torrential rain and the ever-present damp. To move from one village to another usually entailed descending a precipitous hillside, crossing a chaung (usually a raging torrent in the monsoon period and a gentle stream at other times), and ascending an equally precipitous hillside to reach the next village. The actual distance by direct line of sight may have been only one mile, but the descent, the chaung crossing and the subsequent ascent could take an entire day. In the rainy season, the narrow paths, at times almost vertical, became so muddy and slippery that mules complete with loads would fall down the khud-side at frequent intervals, tumbling over and over and smashing equipment as they went. Being hardy animals, the mules rarely hurt themselves badly during these falls but their loads were often damaged and the process of rescuing and reloading the unfortunate mule, and then getting it back to the track to resume the march, was exhausting in the extreme. A Brigade War Diary entry at this time gives a vivid picture of these conditions:

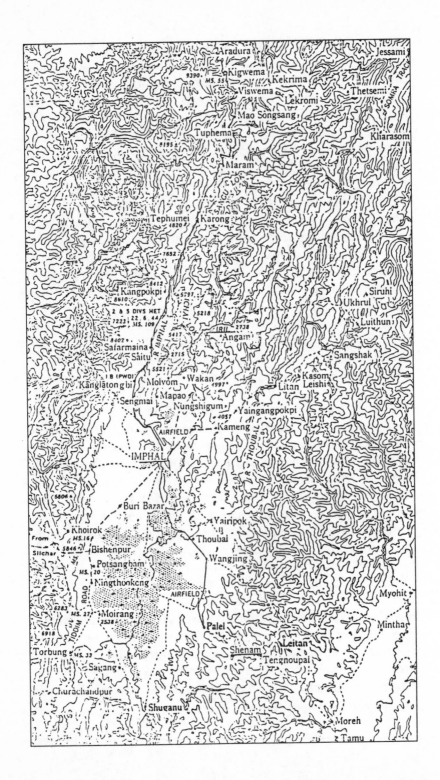

Aradura
Jessami
Kigwema
9390· Kekrima
MS. 55
Viswema
Thetsemi
Lekromi
Mao Songsang
Tuphema
Kharasom
8195·
Maram

Tephumei Karong
1820·

·7652

Kangpokpi 8412· Siruhi
8610· 5797· Ukhrul
2 & 5 DIVS MET 5218· Luithun
7223· MS. 109 22. 6. 44 2738
IRIL· Angam
8402· 5417 2715
Safarmaina Sangshak
Saitu 2715
5521 Kasom
I B (PWD) ·1997 Leishi
Kanglatongbi Molvom ·Wakan Litan
Sengmai Mapao
Nungshigum Yaingangpokpi
·4057
AIRFIELD Kameng

IMPHAL

Buri Bazar

Yairipok
6806· ·B
Khoirok Thoubal
From MS. 16
Silchar 5846· Bishenpur Wangjing
Potsangbam
MS. 20
Ningthonkong AIRFIELD Myohit
6283·
MS. 27 Moirang Mintha
6918· 2538 Palel
Torbung MS. 33 Leitan
Shenam
Sagang Tengnoupal
Churachandpur
Shuganu
Moreh
Tamu

"Hill tracks in a terrible state, either so slippery that men can hardly walk or knee-deep in mud: administrative difficulties considerable: half a company took ten hours to carry two stretcher cases four miles. A party of men without packs took seven hours to cover five miles . . . Whole sections of the road vanished in land-slides: the troops, soaked and filthy, were struggling forward across steep slopes through mud with the consistency of porridge halfway up to their knees."

On Shenam Ridge we had come to a stalemate. The major battle in this sector of the siege was being fought out here, on the Ridge. As day followed night and night followed day, there was little respite. Between 4 and 11 April the enemy put in continuous assaults on the most forward positions holding "Crete" and "Scraggy", while at the same time there was a succession of determined night attacks on "Malta", "Gibraltar" and "Brigade Hill". 1 Devon lost some ground on "Scraggy" and "Crete" and the Japanese penetrated both hilltop positions and consolidated their gains, but a most determined counter-attack by 1 Devon on 11 April restored the situation and the lost ground was once again in our hands.

On the same day two companies of 1 Devon, with air and artillery support, were ordered by Brigadier Greaves to lead a major assault on Nippon Hill. The fighting was desperate and the Devons lost eight officers and eighty men in the attack. Nevertheless they drove the Japanese off the hill, occupied it and consolidated. On the next day the Devons handed over the Nippon Hill positions to 9/12 FFR, who held this vital feature for a week, only to be driven off it by a major Japanese counter-attack. The terrible losses to 1 Devon in their successful assault on 11 April had been for nothing. It was shortly after this that I began to suspect the relationship between Brigadier Sam Greaves and Lt Col Harvester, the CO of 1 Devon, was deteriorating. The Devons, a regular battalion whose original strength consisted mainly of men from the County of Devon who were regular

The contour lines on the map opposite give some idea of the nature of the terrain in the area around Imphal.

soldiers, had suffered terrible casualties in the early stages of the fighting on Shenam Ridge. Lt Col Harvester became more and more protective on behalf of his battalion, which was so depleted that reinforcements (when they arrived) often came not from infantry units but from such units as disbanded LAA Regiments. No doubt our Brigadier was under extreme pressure from the Divisional Commander, Major General Gracey, who in his turn was under pressure from HQ 14 Army to hold the Shenam position at all costs. As a consequence, 1 Devon were often called upon to undertake tasks which resulted in high casualties. This pressure Lt Col Harvester resisted more and more, in an endeavour to shield his men from further extreme casualty figures. At Brigade HQ we became aware of these tensions.

By 14 April 1 Devon had been taken out of the line to occupy the "Reserve Battalion Position" and part of "Gibraltar", where they were expected to have less desperate fighting and the opportunity to recover from their spell in the most forward defended localities. 9/12 FFR took over the forward positions from them and, on 15/16 and 17/18 April, severe enemy attacks were successful in once again penetrating our defences on these two vital hilltops. More ground was lost, but major parts of "Crete" and "Scraggy" still remained in our hands. 9/12 FFR was a young and inexperienced battalion at this time. There was no lacking in bravery and determination but the severity of the enemy assault was such that the young Punjabi Mussulmen and NW Frontiersmen of this battalion only managed to hang on to part of our positions by the narrowest margin.

On the night of 19/20 April three separate Japanese attacks on our forward positions were beaten off. Each of these was supported by medium tanks, which fortunately had difficulty in moving far from the narrow confines of the main Tamu-Palel track. By this time 9/12 FFR had been reinforced by two companies of 3/1 GR and our most vulnerable positions on "Crete" and "Scraggy" were held in the face of these violent assaults. The fighting went on all night without pause and, as dawn came up on the morning of 20 April, the men of 9/12 FFR were clearly exhausted and in need of relief. Casualties were high and evacuation of the wounded was undertaken during the morning, at the same time as the remainder of 3/1 GR moved up to take over the forward positions. Such movement normally took place under cover of darkness but the situation was so acute that the risks of daylight movement were accepted. As a result, heavy enemy shellfire caused additional casualties until counter-battery fire from our own artillery drew the enemy away from the targets on the main track and an artillery duel developed. This enabled 3/1 GR to complete their forward movement, 9/12 FFR established themselves on the Brigade Reserve position and the casualties and dead were evacuated from "Scraggy" by midday.

For the next two days and nights a comparative lull descended on the battle area. Probing attacks were made on "Malta" and "Gibraltar" and periodic artillery fire was maintained, but it was plain that the enemy were as exhausted as our own units. The continuous fighting over long periods was beginning to tell and the pause became inevitable while both sides regrouped and received reinforcements to replace the large number of casualties suffered during the previous three weeks.

As the Subaltern of the Brigade Signal Section, I had spent most of my time, throughout this period, moving between our hilltop positions, trying desperately to maintain the communications that were our responsibility. Sometimes I would be with a line party repairing faults, replacing cable or laying alternative routes. On these excursions, we would quite often bump into enemy patrols and become involved in small actions which would distract us completely from our main purpose for several hours. Work on cable runs near to the main track always tended to bring down shellfire on us by day and so work on the most direct routes to the forward positions was usually carried out at night. I often found myself taking up wireless equipment, batteries, charging equipment and all the associated ancillary bits and pieces to "Scraggy", to replace equipment destroyed or damaged in the heavy fighting there. Because of this constant movement between all the hilltop positions, it was not unusual to find myself unable to get out once I had arrived, because the position came under violent attack while I was there. In these circumstances, it was a small step from "being there" to becoming involved personally, alongside the true "inhabitants", in the defence of the position concerned; and so I found that my previous training and experience as an infantryman proved very useful on numerous occasions during the battle. There were times when I still found myself fighting in a hilltop position two days after arriving for what had been intended as a brief half hour visit to re-establish the wireless link with Brigade HQ.

I have been asked many times how I felt when in action in the close combat situation. The question has always been raised by those who, up to that time, had been fortunate enough not to have had the experience themselves. It is a very personal matter and no doubt to some extent the memory and the reaction are different for each individual. The one thing that is certain is that, in the type of fighting we experienced at Shenam Ridge, the process of "growing up" was accelerated beyond belief for youngsters of my age at the time. The romantic concepts of soldiering which fill the minds of the young and uninitiated are soon banished by the stark reality and horror of it all. Ideas of personal heroism, winning medals, fighting for the "right cause" and the basic belief that others may be killed or wounded but "it can never happen to me", were soon put in perspective as adolescent dreams, to be replaced by the basic instincts of survival. More often than not the killing was at a distance of 50 to 100 yards and this longer range made the whole matter more impersonal. The enemy was a figure in the gunsight and was somehow not a human when he fell. With hand-to-hand close combat it was a very different matter. Everything happened so quickly that there was little immediate fear; more a determination to survive by killing the enemy and afterwards a feeling of enormous relief and very little thought for the human you had killed. Fear came in retrospect, when thinking about what had passed. During the actual encounter, things were done by instinct in response to the very thorough training we had all been given in hand-to-hand fighting and an enormous amount of luck was also involved. We helped one another by instinct and the so-called "bravery" for which medals are given did not really come into it at all. It was just a matter of survival and killing by instinct and training – and frankly little to be proud of but a lot to be thankful for afterwards. The relief we felt after close combat was the selfish thankfulness to have come through unscathed and this was tempered by retrospective fear and horror. It is perhaps fortunate that there was usually so much to do immediately following an incident, concerned mainly with clearing up and preparing for another attack, that one had little time to dwell on the experiences of the immediate past.

As the weeks passed into months and we became more and more experienced as fighting soldiers, I noticed in myself an increasing reluctance to participate whole-heartedly in the fighting. One had to force oneself more and more to over-come anticipatory fear and to give example to others. I came to realize that the more combat-experienced a soldier becomes, the more he has to tussle with himself to overcome his natural fears; but these difficulties are accentuated before and after the period of action and, during the actual fighting (whether through the gunsight or hand-to-hand), there is no time to dwell on such thoughts, because everything happens so fast that one becomes totally absorbed in the desperate struggle to sur-vive, to help one's comrades and not to be overcome by the enemy. Above all other memories and sensations, there remains a feeling of horror, of the unreality of the stark reality of it all and a deep, selfish thankfulness to have survived. I remember also the amazing strength of character and comradeship of my companions in such extreme adversity. I recall getting into the "Scraggy" position with a replacement charging engine one day at the height of an enemy attack on the perimeter. My point of entry was remote from the main assault and, although the whole area was under shellfire, I had no real difficulty in get-ting through the wire by the route I had chosen. Because of the intensity of the shelling, I took shelter for a moment in the first dug-out I came across. Once through the narrow entrance and when my eyes had become accustomed to the gloom, I realized that I had stumbled into the Regimental Aid Post. The earth floor of this large underground accommodation was thickly packed with wounded soldiers of 1 Devon, many close to death. The memory is still vivid and, above all else, I recall the grey-green pallor of those shocked and badly injured men and their quiet, stoic acceptance of the situation. There was no com-plaint; they lay in complete silence near to death, waiting with patience for their turn to be tended by the Regimental Medical

Officer and his Orderly. More casualties were being carried in all the time and for some there was little that the RMO could do. I realized that, because of the numbers, some would have a long wait for attention and in many cases the wait would be too long. As I left again to make for the wireless dug-out on the hill, I took with me not only an impression of the horror of that charnel house but also a deep feeling of amazement and pride at the quiet courage of these men from my own home county of Devon.

The lull that had begun on the afternoon of 20 April lasted no more than 36 hours. During this period patrol activity continued and there were frequent artillery exchanges, but the Japanese made no full-scale attacks on our positions. There was an opportunity to strengthen defences and clear up some of the mess. Casualties were evacuated to the rear, we buried our dead and some reinforcements arrived from the Imphal Plain to replace a proportion of the losses we had incurred up to this time. Most important of all, rest and sleep became a possibility for some. At night repairs and improvements were made to the main track so that jeeps could continue to use it. A massive canvas screen was erected during darkness to conceal movement of men and vehicles in the area of "Brigade Hill" and "Artillery Hill" from the enemy positions on Tengnoupal Peak. From this time on, damage to the screen from enemy shellfire was repaired each night. This contraption was of high value as, before the screen was erected, much of the movement of supplies and reinforcements from 20 Division had been observed by OPs on Tengnoupal. The speed of response of enemy artillery fire to movement along this part of the ridge was remarkable and there is no doubt that the screen saved lives and supplies. It became possible to move vehicles and men in daylight as far forward as the eastern end of the "Gibraltar" feature without enemy artillery response. From there further forward, movement in vehicles to "Malta" and "Scraggy" in daylight was only possible by running the gauntlet of enemy shellfire and was a risky business. Fire from enemy heavy mortars could reach as far as the eastern half of the "Malta" feature, but the western end of "Malta", all the "Gibraltar" feature and areas further west had an easier time as, although these areas suffered heavy shelling, they were free from the additional hazards of mortar fire. "Scraggy" and "Crete" took all the punishment the enemy could offer.

An hour before dawn on 22 April the enemy began ferocious and determined attacks on "Crete", "Scraggy" and "Malta". These three separate assaults were closely coordinated and supported by heavy shell and mortar fire. After very heavy fighting, which continued without pause well into the day, parts of our positions were overrun but the enemy had suffered too heavily to be able to continue and their attacks faded away for the moment. A very large number of enemy dead remained, both inside and on the immediate approaches to our positions. By the evening of that day the situation had been completely restored. Apart from the mounds of dead, we were again as we had been before the attacks began. In this way the battle of attrition continued, with the Japanese like waves breaking on the rocks that were our hill-top positions.

Away from the major battle on the ridge, a new factor had been introduced into the fighting in this sector. For the first time the enemy brought into action formations of the so-called "Indian National Army" of Subhas Chandra Bose. Their popular name amongst our troops was "Jiffs" and they were mainly soldiers of the old Indian Army who had been captured by the Japanese during the first Burma campaign in 1942, when the enemy had defeated us in Malaya, Singapore and Burma and had overrun the country as far as the eastern banks of the River Chindwin. The Jiffs had little heart for the fight and it is probable that the majority of them had joined the Japanese not as traitors but as unfortunates who saw this was the best chance of returning home to India. Once engaged in action with us, urged on by the Japanese, they surrendered in droves. Unfortunately our own loyal Indian and Gurkha soldiers had little sympathy with them and special orders had to be issued to prevent wholesale slaughter of the Jiffs even when they had laid down their arms. An even greater problem was to sort them out so that true traitors were treated as such and loyal soldiers trying to return to India and their parent units received just treatment. During the night of 29/30 April the Japanese used the Jiff units for a dangerous infiltration attack on Palel airfield which was our main supply and reinforcement link with the outside world during the siege. The attack was beaten off and all the Japanese involved were killed, but many of the Jiffs were only too ready to surrender at the first opportunity. They were roughly handled by our defending troops, but seemed overjoyed to have fallen into our hands. After this incident the Japanese used Jiffs less and less as fighting formations and eventually these unfortunates ended up as porters, indeed almost as "beasts of burden" for the enemy.

During this period our patrols described to us an illuminating facet of the Japanese character which did not cause surprise but which again emphasized their disregard for the necessity of logistic back-up, the support needs of their troops and the handling of animals as beasts of burden. We found that the enemy used a variety of animals as means of transport. Mules, horses, donkeys, cattle and elephants were all put to use. Whereas we were meticulous in standards of saddlery for our mules and never worked animals unless they were completely fit and regularly fed and watered, the Japanese worked their animal transport until they dropped with exhaustion or starvation. Saddlery was for the most part non-existent. Loads were tied to the end of ropes which rested over the animal's bodies; the need to balance loads on either side – considered by us as essential – was ignored and the rope securing the loads was allowed to cut deep into the back of the unfortunate animals. As a result their life as effective beasts of burden was extremely short and no doubt much pain and suffering was endured by these unfortunate creatures before they were either shot or turned loose as useless by the Japanese. As a consequence, supplies carried by animal transport dwindled as the battle continued week after week. The success of the Japanese attack depended upon their capture of our extensive supply dumps on the Imphal Plain and, as time went by, the effectiveness of the attacking force was bound to diminish, in spite of the extreme bravery and determination of the individual soldiers. It became apparent that no medical back-up was provided and wounded Japanese were often left to fend for themselves without treatment. The most important logistic back-up maintained by the enemy was resupply of ammunition and replacement weapons. The welfare, health and comfort of their own soldiers were very low on the scale of priorities.

Throughout all our time on Shenam Ridge we were beset by minor personal problems of a mundane nature which nevertheless had a cumulative adverse effect on our morale and also contributed to our exhaustion as the weeks passed. For much of the time it was impossible to wash and shave with any regularity and we went for long periods without these fundamental necessities. A complete bath was unheard of and we became very dirty and unkempt as the weeks grew into months. It was also difficult to attend to the fundamental needs of nature and we were often obliged to restrain ourselves through sheer necessity, with the result that constipation became common. Those of us who occasionally suffered from forms of dysentery were worse off. Lack of personal cleanliness, difficulties with bowel function and such associated problems led to a lowering of morale and self-respect. Efforts were made to establish Mobile Laundry and Bath Units (MLBU) to the rear of Brigade Headquarters and those troops who came out of the forward positions for a brief spell of rest were given as much opportunity as possible to avail themselves of these crude facilities. However, the tactical situation of this continuing battle for Shenam permitted only rare visits to the MLBUs and one was lucky to have a complete body shower more than once in a month.

After the heavy fighting of 22 April, during which both the enemy and ourselves suffered very heavy casualties, it became evident that the enemy had suffered too heavily to be able to continue and, for the moment, their attacks faded away. For the next two or three days, apart from the attack on Palel Airstrip, there was a lull in this sector of the battle. We again had the opportunity to replenish our supplies and ammunition, evacuate casualties and clean up the mess from the previous fighting. A slight change of emphasis occurred on the night of 2/3 May, when the Japanese not only attacked the forward positions on "Scraggy" in much the same way as before, but also put in very heavy attacks on the more rearward positions of "Malta" and

"Gibraltar". They were still including elements of the Indian National Army in their attacking forces at this stage and, particularly on 3 May and for several days thereafter, a large number of these Jiffs attempted to surrender to the defenders of these two hill features. It was again necessary to issue special orders to Gurkha and Indian troops to allow these surrendering Jiffs to become prisoners without maltreatment and to ensure that our own troops did not kill them unless the circumstances justified it by treacherous behaviour when appearing to surrender.

The battle renewed in intensity on the night of 6/7 May and each night until 11 May with determined attacks by the Japanese, particularly on our forward positions. Most of "Crete" and "Scraggy" were overrun and we lost some ground on "Malta" and "Gibraltar". A series of counter-attacks on 12 May by 1 Devon and 9/12 FFR eventually restored the situation which then stabilized, as both sides were so exhausted that they had fought themselves to a standstill. This stalemate continued for a further week during which the only activity was by patrols, although daily exchanges of artillery fire continued. On 20 May we heard at last that we were to be relieved by a brigade of 23 Division and were to withdraw from the Shenam Ridge. We had been in action continuously for nine weeks and the Brigade as a whole was in a very weakened condition and in need of a short rest to accept reinforcements, reorganize and refurbish. If this had not been possible the effectiveness of the Brigade as a fighting force would have been doubtful.

The last battalion of 80 Brigade to be withdrawn from Shenam was 3/1 GR. On 28 May the Battalion retook the part of "Scraggy" known as Lynch's Pimple which was still in Jap hands. I happened to be on the hill when this desperate scrap started, being there to tidy up loose ends for the handover of communications responsibilities to the incoming Brigade. 'B' Company of 3/1 GR led the attack, during which the Company Commander, Major J. Darby, was killed in the early stages of the action. The Commanding Officer, Lt Col C.M.H. Wingfield, DSO, MVO, went forward and immediately took over personal direction of the attack. He rallied the Gurkhas of

106

'B' company and they responded magnificently. With great sadness we learnt that Colonel Wingfield was killed outright by a Jap sniper as the position was won, a great loss to the Battalion and to the Brigade. I have never forgotten this day, not only because of the outstanding courage of Colonel Wingfield and his Gurkhas but also because 28 May 1944 was my 21st birthday.

By 29 May we had managed to withdraw from the Ridge. The process of disengagement from Shenam was protracted, difficult and dangerous, for throughout this period the attacks on our hilltop positions by the Japanese were renewed. For some days HQ 80 Brigade commanded battalions from the relieving Brigade as well as the remaining elements of the normal command. Eventually we succeeded in extricating ourselves from this dreadful area of death and destruction and felt the extreme relief of peace and relative security away from the fighting. We found ourselves in a harbour area close to the village of Wanjing, midway between Palel and the town of Imphal and well away from the fighting. Here we received many reinforcements flown in from India and the battalions were once again at reasonable strength, although most of the reinforcements were transfers from disbanded anti-aircraft regiments of the Royal Artillery, with no experience of fighting as infantry soldiers. We also replenished weapons and ammunition at Wangjing and received a full complement of mules, which indicated to us all that our next task as a Brigade would be away from motorable tracks and that we would be in for a lot of marching.

The Iril Valley Operation

After the rest period of one week in this small village, the Brigade moved to an area close to Sawombung, to the north-east of Imphal, and harboured at the side of the main track leading from Imphal to the large village of Ukhrul, some fifty miles away in the Naga hills. The remainder of 20 Division took over the defended localities facing the Japanese astride the Ukhrul track. A battery of 25 Mountain Regiment, Indian Artillery, joined the Brigade. The battery was armed with pack howitzers

107

of the type that were carried in bits on mules and which could be assembled and brought into action in an incredibly short space of time by the highly trained gunners of the Regiment. Mules arrived for all units to replace casualties from previous actions. Several elephants also joined the Brigade as additional animal transport.

The monsoon rains were falling by this time and the continuous torrential downpour soon turned the harbour area into a quagmire. The locality became known as "Mudbox" – a most suitable name – and preparations for the coming operation became more and more unpleasant as each day passed.

On 6 June 1944 an "O" Group revealed the details and objectives of the task that had been allotted to 80 Brigade. The Brigade was to move up the Iril Valley from "Mudbox" and into the Naga Hills, thence to encircle the Japanese Division facing the other two Brigades of 20 Division; the Ukhrul track was to be cut behind the enemy and the Brigade was to attack them from the rear with the object of destroying them as an effective fighting force. A secondary objective was to cut enemy east/west supply lines along jungle paths, to deny resupply, by animal transport convoys, of the Japanese forces astride the main Dimapur Road running northwards from Imphal to Kohima and beyond.

It was imperative, particularly in the early stages, that the move of 80 Brigade up the Iril Valley was not detected by the enemy. As a consequence, a series of night marches were planned and the Brigade was to lie up during each day in concealed positions in the jungle. Casualty evacuation by pack elephant would only be possible during the first few days of the operation, after which the wounded and sick would either be carried with the force or left to fend for themselves. Radio silence would be maintained until contact had been made with the enemy or until it became necessary to call up the first air supply drop.

The Brigade prepared to march out of their positions in "Mudbox" as soon as darkness fell on 7 June 1944.

The following is an extract from the Brigade Signal Section War Diary written at the time:-

Date, Place, Time	Summary of Events and Information	Remarks
		Cipher Staff Lieut. J. Dougan Sgt. Bew Sgt. Bolden L/Cpl. Beckenham Bde Signal Officer – Capt. 'Daddy' Major (OC) Lt. R.P.D. Painter (2ic) Sgt. Hirst – Section Sgt
Night 7–8 June '44 Iril Valley Sawombung-Purrum	The march on the first night was from base at Sawombung to a village named PURRUM, a distance of about fifteen miles. Heavy rain and swamps and pitch darkness made this march difficult. During daylight of the 8th June the Brigade lay up in concealed positions and rested in preparation for the next move. Sleep was however, made impossible by the heavy rainfall with no cover and discomfort was increased by the persistence of numerous leeches which infested the swampy ground. A line detachment of 20 Div Signals laid a line behind the Brigade up to Purrum with the intention of following up the march to the primary objective. This line was a complete failure, due mainly to the conditions on the route, and was abandoned shortly afterwards.	
Night 8–9 June '44 Purrum – Samusong	After a day's rest, the Brigade moved once more as soon as darkness fell, and marched throughout the night to arrive the next morning at a village named Samusong. W/T silence was maintained, and for this the Signal Section was grateful, as it meant that rest was possible for all during the day.	
Night 9 –10 June '44 Iril Valley Samusong – Molkon	The Brigade moved as darkness fell and marched on up the Iril Valley. By this time the enemy forward positions were well behind and contact with them had been avoided, although a party of 300 had been through the village of Purrum about twelve hours previous to the	

Date, Place, Time	Summary of Events and Information	Remarks

Brigade's arrival. After a troublesome march through the night the Brigade arrived at Molkon Village, the area of which was the primary objective. Up to this time the move had been so secretly conducted that the enemy was in complete ignorance of the fact that a Brigade, with a battery of Mountain Artillery, had penetrated well to their rear and was sitting astride their L of C.

June 10–22
<u>Molkon Ridge</u>

Brigade Headquarters and the Section, together with 3/1 GR and Battery 23 Mountain Regiment, moved onto a ridge overlooking Molkon village. The 9/12 FFR moved on to Chawai, in the hills to the NE of Molkon and about six miles distance up extremely steep gradients. Here they were to cut the track running through Chawai and provide an O.P. for the artillery firing from Brigade Headquarters area. The 1st Devons arrived and concentrated in the area of Molkon village during late afternoon of the 10th June. This battalion had been affording flank and rear protection to the whole Brigade group throughout the march up the Iril Valley and it was mainly through their efforts that the whole force succeeded in reaching its primary objective unseen and unheard by the enemy.

On establishing Brigade Headquarters on Molkon Ridge W/T silence was broken and communications were established with battalions, and with 20 Div. on two links. As 3/1st GR were with Brigade Headquarters on Molkon Ridge, no communications with them were

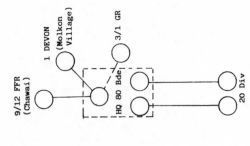

110

Date, Place, Time	Summary of Events and Information	Remarks
	necessary at this stage. On the evening of June 10th, the first air supply drop was carried out successfully although W/T to aircraft was not established. Shortly after this, first contact with the enemy was made by a patrol of 1 Devon: it was evident that the enemy's attention had been attracted by the supply aircraft. The first casualty of the operation was incurred by this patrol, the officer (Captain Roddy Young) being killed. 1 Devon moved later to a position to the South of Chawai, where more enemy were encountered, most of whom were L of C troops who appeared to be taken completely by surprise.	
June 12–13	On the 12th June the 9/12 FFR reported by wireless a large enemy mule convoy moving towards Chawai. This was promptly shelled by the guns of 23 Mountain Regiment with satisfactory results, and later was finished off by 9/12 FFR. During this period at Molkon Ridge, all communications were satisfactory with one exception; the charging engine with 1 Devon detachment became u/s and two attempts to get a new charging engine to them failed as a result of the extremely difficult march to this battalion position. Eventually on the third attempt a charging engine reached the detachment with 1 Devon and communications were re-established immediately, as a fully charged	On 18 June Lieut. Berwick, I.S.C. arrived with an escort from 20 Div. to take over as Cipher Officer from Lieut. Dougan I.S.C who was sick, and who left for the rear on 19th June '44.
June 15–23	battery was taken up with the engine. With the exception of this break, communications were maintained 24 hours in 24 during this operation. The Signal Section, with Brigade Headquarters, remained on Molkon Ridge without incident, until 22nd June 1944.	

111

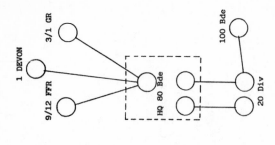

23 June '44
Molkon –
Yangnoi

On the 22nd June orders were received for the move onwards into the hills towards Ukhrul. On the morning of the 23rd June Brigade HQ and the Section moved, in torrential rain, across the Iril River and climbed the hills through Chawai to the village of Yangnoi. This march of eight miles took ten hours, illustrating the difficulties encountered. In spite of numerous falls down the hillsides, no mules were lost and all mule loads arrived at Yangnoi intact. Throughout the night 23rd–24th June communications were maintained to three battalions and to 20 Div. as shown on the diagram. Battalions located as follows: 1 Devon in previous position; 3/1 GR at river crossing between Yangnoi and Mollen and 9/12 FFR in village of Leishan.

24 June '44
Yangnoi – River
crossing

On the 24th June Brigade HQ and the Section moved downhill to the river crossing between Yangnoi and Mollen. This was a very short march and constituted a rest day; communications satisfactory. 1 Devon moved to Chawai and 3/1 GR remained at river crossing with Brigade HQ, while 9/12 FFR were still located at Leishan. The entire Brigade group was thus moving along the Japanese L of C from Ukhrul to the main Dimapar-Imphal road, with 9/12 FFR in the lead and 1 Devon forming a rearguard; 9/12 FFR meeting slight resistance from enemy L of C troops as they pushed forward through Leishan towards the east.

Date, Place, Time	Summary of Events and Information
25 June '44 River crossing – Mollen	Once again in torrential rain the Brigade HQ and Signal Section moved, behind 3/1 GR, to Mollen, the 3/1 GR continuing to Leishan on the same day. No communications were maintained on the move, but sets were opened during every long halt and communications established and maintained throughout the night, following the days marching. This routine proved exhausting for W/T operators but was nevertheless maintained with success. The night 25th–26th June at Mollen afforded little rest for the men as the torrential downpour continued, and no shelter was available.
26 June '44 Mollen – Leishan	On 26th June, Brigade HQ with the Section marched from Mollen to Leishan, arriving there in the evening in fine weather. The village of Leishan is at a height of over 5000 ft and at this time was above the monsoon clouds. From Leishan the Brigade group split up, the 3/1 GR marching south towards Shongphel and the 9/12 FFR maintaining the advance eastwards towards Khuntak. 1 Devon was at this time still acting as rearguard. Communications from Leishan to HQ 20 Div., a distance of fifty miles, proved to be first class, voice communications being maintained at strength 5/5 throughout the night (sets in use were WS No. 22, both as rear links and on forward tactical group).
27 June '44 Leishan – Khuntak	With the 9/12 FFR immediately in front of Brigade HQ and Signals, the march to the east was continued on 27th June 1944, the objective for the day being Khuntak, a village at the height of over 6000 ft,

113

Date, Place, Time	Summary of Events and Information	Remarks
	separated from Leishan by a deep valley. During the final climb to Khuntak the column encountered the enemy in force and the 9/12 FFR attacked and drove the enemy out of Khuntak and the neighbouring village of Sururukong. Brigade HQ and Signals with a Company of 9/12 FFR remained in Khuntak for the night of 27th–28th June, while the 9/12 FFR less one company occupied Sururukong. The enemy, who had withdrawn to the south along track Sururukong – Shongphel, had taken up positions astride this track. With them was a large mule supply convoy probably intended for the Japanese forces astride the Dimapur Road and facing Kohima far to the west. Communications were maintained satisfactorily throughout the night with the 3 battalions and HQ 20 Div.	
28th June '44 Khuntak – Sururukong	The next day, on 28th June, Brigade HQ moved the short distance from Khuntak to Sururukong and there joined the 9/12 FFR. The 3/1 GR meanwhile were engaging the enemy in the area of Shongphel, to the south. Brigade HQ was established in an ideal position from the point of view of wireless, as Sururukong was situated on the top of a hill, 7000 ft above sea level. Village huts in good condition afforded excellent shelter for wireless sets, signal office and living quarters. Communications with HQ 20 Div. on both rear link W/T sets were almost 100% perfect – voice strength 5/5 for 24 hours in 24. Communications on tactical group to battalions proved equally successful. Main disadvantage at Sururukong was the prevalence of	

114

Date, Place, Time   *Summary of Events and Information*

fleas and lice which troubled all ranks. Brigade HQ and the Signal Section remained in the village of Sururukong from the 28th June to the morning of 6th July while all three battalions went into action against the enemy attempting to retreat along the main Imphal – Ukhrul road. 100 Brigade were at this time pressing the enemy back from the Imphal Plain and forcing them to retreat towards 80 Brigade, which had cut the main road in their rear.

While at Sururukong a new W/T group was attempted, the object of which was to establish and maintain communications with other Brigades and formations closing in on Ukhrul from the N.W. This proved unsuccessful and was later abandoned.

Remarks

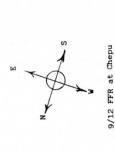

115

Interlude at Sururukong

28 June – 5 July
Sururukong and after

This week of relative rest at Sururukong proved to be a tonic for us all at Brigade Headquarters. The cold atmosphere and the brief break from eternal marching over impossible country did a great deal to put us on our feet again and prepare us for the next phase of the operation.

1 Devon had a three-day rest with us before moving on to Lambui, and they needed it. The indescribable conditions we were all experiencing were beginning to tell on the reinforcements fresh from home who, at this time, made up such a large proportion of the Devons, following their heavy casualties at Shenam Ridge. On one occasion this battalion was marching over very difficult country and as a consequence progress was slow. The Brigade Commander, Brigadier Sam Greaves, went out with his two Gurkha bodyguards and in one afternoon caught up with the Devons, found out for himself what difficulties were holding them up, amended his plans on the spot and returned to Brigade Headquarters late on the same evening. He had no mule column to delay him and was naturally travelling light but nevertheless this feat serves to show what kind of man we had to lead us. With only two men as escort and every inch of the way likely to contain parties of hostile Japanese, he completed a march the thought of which would have dismayed a man of half his age.

Air supply drops restocked us with stores and equipment and for once we fed well at Sururukong. A makeshift field hospital was established in a large village hut and our mule-carried Field Ambulance set to work on the casualties. Evacuation was out of the question at this stage of the operation and, because of this, a large number of wounded and sick were accumulated at Sururukong and left with an escort until a later date when, by elephant, mule, and stretcher bearer, they were carried down to the Ukhrul Road, and thence by jeep ambulance to Imphal. Later we were to meet again the American Ambulance Service (AVAS) who undertook this very difficult evacuation of our casualties. In the Burma war the USA provided considerable support in the

116

air, but the ground forces were made up almost exclusively of British, Indian, Gurkha and African formations, the only US Army contingent being "Merrill's Marauders" – a formation of brigade strength employed in Northern Burma in a role akin to that of our Chindits. The men of the Volunteer Ambulance Service were all from the USA and were conscientious objectors who refused to fight. They were all very brave men, however, and many of our wounded survived as a direct result of the selfless dedication of this small band of pacifist volunteers. They would frequently recover wounded under fire and of necessity lived in much the same difficult conditions as the rest of us. Many of them died in their endeavours to save the lives of others. Their special type of heroism has not been widely publicized but should not be forgotten.

Meanwhile at Sururukong, preparations were being made for an onward move. The climax of the operation was near and soon 80 Brigade would be completely astride the only line of retreat towards the east that the Japanese, then facing Imphal on the Ukhrul Road, had left to take.

An amusing incident occurred while we were at Sururukong. Perhaps it would be more accurate to say that what happened was amusing in retrospect but could easily have ended in a most tragic way. During the supply drops, the Dakota aircraft would fly low over our position and drop our supplies by parachute, aiming at the marked "Dropping Zone" or DZ. From time to time they would also indulge in an occasional "free drop" without parachutes, depositing upon us such items as rice and animal feed heavily enclosed in gunny sacks. When this happened, the goods would shower down upon us as though we were being subjected to a bombing run and the sacks would hit the ground on or near the DZ with a resounding thud. Any unfortunate who was in the way could easily be killed by "free fall" air supply of this nature, so we all kept well clear of the target area and the goods were collected together after the aircraft had completed the run. Now it happened that our Brigadier had a personal eccentricity. This was that he insisted that his own thunderbox, a folding wooden contraption, was carried on a mule with other stores and was set up for his use whenever we stopped for a reasonable period. His Gurkha orderly would be

117

responsible for digging a suitable hole, erecting the thunderbox and building a shelter of jungle foliage around it to provide the privacy to which a Brigadier should be entitled. The shelter even had a shingle thatched roof to give some protection from the rain. The siting of this personal facility was left to the orderly and he usually found a good spot away from prying eyes but safe within the all-round defensive positions. At Sururukong space was limited and the "little hut" was sited close to the DZ. One day the Brigadier was seen to emerge, tightening his trouser belt and adjusting his dress as he walked back to the Brigade Headquarters, just as a "free fall" supply drop started across the DZ. He was about ten yards from his thunderbox when a gunny sack of rice went straight through the roof of the shack and completely demolished it and the apparatus within. We wondered at the time how far down the hole the Brigadier would have been rammed had he still been on the throne, but he was unimpressed by the whole incident and walked away without showing the slightest reaction.

On 6 July Brigade Headquarters, the Signal Section, Mountain Artillery Regiment and those of the Field Ambulance who were not left behind, marched out of Sururukong for Ringui, a village within view on the far side of a deep valley, about two miles away as the crow flies but separated from us by a deep valley which made the march a good twelve miles in distance, and involved climbing down an almost sheer precipice for 2000 ft with a climb of more than 2000 ft to go up on the other side. Rain was falling continuously, the path was very slippery and no more than a foot wide, and the floor of the valley was inevitably a swampy jungle. Our main trouble on this march was with the mules. Every few hundred yards throughout the day a mule would slip on the glassy surface of the narrow path, and down he would fall, crashing over and over through the thick jungle until, maybe 100 ft below, he would come to rest wedged against a tree, bruised and breathless. Gathering a few tired men together to help us, we would climb down the steep jungle slope, some to rescue the poor mule, get him back onto the path and resaddle him, some to search for and rescue the precious load of wireless equipment, without which we would have been deprived of air supply and would have become a starved and helpless band of men. Having found the load, we would be faced with the exhausting work of carrying it up the sheer hillside to the path once more, there to check it and estimate the damage, reload the mule and try to catch up the column which by this time would be well ahead. To march the distance unencumbered was tiring enough but, with incidents such as this occurring continuously throughout the day, it is small wonder that complete exhaustion was a result. In spite of these conditions, the men somehow managed to summon up the strength to fight off Japanese attacks during and after such a march.

They operated their wireless sets, transmitting and receiving messages throughout the night, when as often as not they knew that the next day would mean another march, followed by another night on the wireless set. In spite of all this they continued to do the job efficiently and without grumble, not just for a few days but for weeks on end. One of my men, who did not take to grumbling, once said, "This ain't fighting bloody Japs; it's fighting bloody nature!" and expressed the feeling we all had. Somehow the actual battle with the enemy was only a small part of the difficulties we faced. When a man had to put up with being perpetually wet through, with festering jungle sores, with the unpleasantness of leeches attaching themselves to any part of his body, with ticks and fleas, exhaustion, the stink of rotting corpses, with marching over indescribable country, with mosquitos, snakes, and steamy jungle, is it to be wondered at that the ever-present danger of the Japanese became sometimes a secondary consideration? And that danger, that feeling of tension, was with us for most of the time, just as it was for the enemy. For a time it had been thought that the Japanese soldier was a veritable superman, capable of taking in his stride all that the jungle could offer. Some considered that it was only our superiority in equipment that had saved us from defeat at Imphal; but this was not a war of advanced technology and sophisticated machines – no flame-throwing tank can operate on a track a foot wide. This was a competition in endurance, plain down-to-earth physical endurance, and the British and Indian soldier proved to himself that he was as good as, and better than, his Japanese adversary in this competition.

We staggered into the village of Ringui. The march was over, but the real work was about to begin. The directing mind of this operation needed to know how the fight was going, had to make his plans accordingly, had to issue his orders, had to demand food and ammunition for his men, had to report the situation to his superior, arrange for supplies to be dropped by parachute and decide where they were to be dropped; a million and one things had to be done. The work of the Signal Section began in earnest. Wireless communications were established with our detachments in battalions, with division. Messages began to pour into Brigade Headquarters. The directing mind knew now what the situation was, could issue his orders, could send help to those who needed it, could demand food and ammunition and arrange where it was to be dropped, could tell his superior how the situation stood. A body cannot work without its nerves, but now the nerves were working, and so the body worked. Communications have been established!

But what of the equipment which fell down the hillside during the march today and was smashed? The Instrument Mechanic (IM) started his work. He would probably work throughout the night repairing a wireless set. Of course we carried spares but they would not last for ever. Some of the kit was smashed beyond repair, but that had been dealt with. A message was sent off to Division asking for immediate replacements to be dropped by aircraft the next day. A moment's relaxation? But what about the mules? They had to be groomed, fed, watered; their bruises and cuts needed patching up; and the old grey one who broke his leg just before we arrived; thank God we had a good veterinary officer; he would see to that. The saddlery had to be cleaned and mended and I gave thanks for N.C.O.s who knew their responsibilities and their jobs. Surely a moment or two now to rest? But no, what about those batteries we had used throughout the previous night. They were flat now and would have to be put on charge for the next six hours; and one charging engine was smashed beyond repair when the old grey mule broke his leg. We would just have to manage somehow on what we had. There was an hour left before stand to and darkness; we would have to get a move on with digging; we thanked God for those village huts, although the Naga villagers would not be very pleased to find bunkers and slit trenches all over the floor of their living rooms! At least it would mean that the men did not have to dig in the pouring rain; but we had to get on fast with the digging as the Japanese had mountain artillery nearby. The need to get under the ground became the priority, and the job was soon done. A message came in from our detachment with 3/1 GR. Their charging engine had been smashed by a mortar shell that day and they only had batteries to last the night. "Volunteers to take a brace of batteries to the 3/1 GR. I'll arrange for a new engine to be dropped by air tomorrow. Well done, Menon, I can always bank on you. An escort is arranged, you only have an hour of daylight left and it will take you three hours to get there. I will warn them to expect you, so you won't be fired on. Saddle up one of the mules, No. 6 will do, he looks fitter than the rest. Have a mug of tea before you go, Menon. Come back here first light tomorrow and bring the discharged batteries with you. I will have a guide to bring you on if we leave. Deliver the goods, tell them to expect a charging engine by air tomorrow, watch for Japs and good luck".

"Brigade Commander's conference in ten minutes, Sir," and so it went on. What I have just written is fairly typical of our activities every evening, on completion of a day's marching and fighting. As the weeks passed, we all began to feel very tired.

There are many worse places on this earth than Ringui, and we realized this fact when we arrived on that evening of 6 July, '44. We at least had a straw roof over our heads and the fleas were not as numerous as in other places we had known. Contrary to expectation we did not move on the next day. In fact we did not move on until 14 July; but much was to happen during the week following our arrival. In the first place we were situated on so narrow a ridge that supplies had to be dropped from the air onto our positions and if you have ever dodged a sack full of bully beef or mortar ammunition hurtling down from the sky you will understand the problem; but such things were mere incidentals. The new charging engine with the 3/1 GR had itself been wrecked and communications with them were once again shaky. On 9 July I loaded up two mules, one with an engine and a new battery and the second with two batteries, all of which had been successfully dropped by aircraft on the previous day, and set out with a small escort for the 3/1 GR. We did not know their exact location and were well aware that anything could be expected en route. A break in the continuous downpour made us very grateful and we climbed the towering ridge to Shongphel without incident. In the village of Shongphel the signs of battle were plentiful, but, not having time to bury the dead or even to look closely, we hurried through the wreckage and smell and, after three hours of marching, reached a reasonably wide track along which it was quite comfortable to walk. After fifteen minutes my two forward scouts reported smoke from cooking fires and what appeared to them to be a Japanese bivouac area. On closer investigation, however, it proved to be 3/1 GR and, having delivered the charging engine and batteries and loaded up with the smashed equivalents, we ate a hasty meal and set out on our return journey. The path on this side of the ridge up to Shongphel was nearly vertical and, knowing this, I wanted to get to the top as soon as possible to avoid being caught by rain which would inevitably come. Our luck was not in, however, and as we left the wide path for the upward climb the rain came down in torrents. Four and half hours of tugging, pushing, swearing, slipping and almost weeping got us to the top of the ridge, very nearly drowned but nevertheless intact. Going down the other side was an experience reminiscent of tobogganing, but was not without its incident. A slightly wounded mule, without saddle and looking very lost, came from the jungle and seeing our two mules, fell into line behind and followed us all the way back to Ringui; we adopted him, tended his wound and he replaced the old grey we had shot previously.

It was during this march that I realized to the full and from personal experience how the tide was turning against the Japanese. It was evident that we were beginning to win the battle for Imphal. Along the various tracks we covered during the march we kept stumbling upon the emaciated bodies of Japanese soldiers. These showed signs of starvation, undressed wounds and indications that they had crawled towards the east for as far as their strength could take them and had then just fallen by the wayside and died. We found some who were unconscious but not yet dead; there was little or nothing we could do for them. From past experience, we treated them with extreme caution, for we knew that a spark of life could lead to a suicidal grenade

122

explosion finally killing the Japanese soldier and taking us with him if we were too near. We supposed that the lack of logistic support, in the shape of food and medical treatment, had at last proved too much to bear. Evidently the wounded had been told to make their own way back into Burma without help or treatment. Those who were alive and still fit were as dangerous as ever but we actually began to take prisoners – something that had been unheard of up to now. I was not alone in my experience of these signs. Reports were coming in, from patrols and from other formations over a wide area, which confirmed the general trend of disintegration. We still found fighting to be extremely hard and the bitter resistance of organized Japanese units continued in the brave and determined style to which we had become accustomed; but it seemed that no help was being given to the starving and the injured, who were being left to fend for themselves. We began to see a possible end to the siege and to realize that victory was in sight.

On our return, we found Brigade Headquarters in a state of feverish excitement. 3/1 GR were attacked in strength just after we left them, but they had beaten off the attempt. 9/12 FFR had cut the Ukhrul road and a complete Japanese Brigade was caught between us and Imphal. 1 Devon were situated further along the road to the east, waiting to catch any of the Japanese Brigade who succeeded in passing 9/12 FFR. There was no doubt about it, the Japanese were retreating and we had them caught in a trap. The unfortunate 9/12 FFR bore the brunt of the attack by the Japanese Brigade attempting to break out of the ring we had closed around them. In fact, 9/12 were subjected to a continuous onslaught during 10 and 11 July, and lost their C.O. and five officers killed. A wireless message called up two companies of the 3/1 GR to their assistance, the timely arrival of which saved the 9/12 FFR from being overrun. Remnants of the Japanese Brigade scattered into the jungle and attempted to make their way eastward, only to run into the arms of the 1 Devons who took a terrific toll of the enemy at Lambui.

At about this stage of the operation an incident occurred which could have had disastrous consequences and which illustrates the strain imposed upon us all by our circumstances. Brigadier Sam Greaves originated a message to Headquarters

Royal Artillery (HQRA) at 20 Division, warning them that 9/12 FFR would be entering Chepu at dawn one morning and would be engaging the enemy from the rear to catch them in between their frontal opposition from the remainder of 20 Division attacking them from the Saddle and 9/12 FFR attacking them from the east. The worry was that advanced OPs for the medium artillery would see movement in and through Chepu and, assuming this to be Japanese troops, would shell our own 9/12 FFR and cause casualties to our own troops. In spite of this message, which was cleared by wireless to 20 Division, 9/12 FFR were heavily shelled by our own artillery as they attacked Chepu. The Brigadier was incensed by this (fortunately casualties were not as heavy as at first feared) and immediately assumed that his message had been mishandled and had not been cleared to 20 Division. As he had handed it to me personally, I became his immediate target and he placed me under open arrest. Needless to say, I took action on two counts; firstly, I spoke personally by wireless to the CO of 20 Divisional Signals and asked him to take immediate action to stop artillery fire on Chepu; and secondly I asked him to investigate immediately the handling of the original message to HQRA. He generously responded to both these requests in a matter of minutes and then spoke directly to Brigadier Greaves by wireless. The original message had been cleared through to HQRA without delay but they had not actioned it; the fault therefore lay with them and both I and Signals were exonerated. More important, the shelling of Chepu stopped abruptly and 9/12 FFR suffered no further casualties from that source. Brigadier Greaves made a point of apologizing to me personally for his haste in laying the blame at my door and yet again demonstrated what a fine leader he was to us all. The strain of commanding a full infantry Brigade in action under the conditions we were enduring at this time could have been unbearable to a lesser man and yet he found the time to be charming and considerate in making his apology. As a consequence my respect for him increased even more.

By this time we had ten prisoners at Brigade Headquarters, all of whom were in a bad state of repair and seemed to be completely dazed. With these as an unaccustomed additional responsibility, we marched from Ringui on 14 July, once again in pouring rain, to join the 9/12 FFR in Chepu. This was a particularly troublesome march and some equipment was lost. Parties of Japanese stragglers were frequently encountered, but they disappeared into the jungle before we could lay our hands on them. Many of them died of starvation and exhaustion and those who survived were for the most part caught in the end by 1 Devon. Chepu at last, and we met the battered but undaunted 9/12 FFR. Sleeping in the pouring rain, at Chepu we began to realize that the operation was nearly over. Next day, 15 July, we marched to the village of Aishan and there joined the 3/1 GR. Another Brigade moved up after the retreating Japanese and took our place, the 1 Devons were relieved and rejoined us and, with the 9/12 FFR a day's march behind us, we moved on 16 July from Aishan to the Saddle where, on the hills overlooking the Imphal plain, we formed up as a Brigade, rested one day, were welcomed back to the Imphal garrison and, on 18 July, were taken by M.T. – unbelievable dream – to Wanjing, our rest area. And there, needless to say, we rested.

One more operation – the Iril Valley operation – was completed.

The following is a quote from Field Marshal Slim's book *Defeat into Victory* of the siege of Imphal:-

"Results of Imphal – Kohima Battle

(a)   5 Japanese Divisions destroyed as effective fighting formations.

(b)   50,000 Japanese dead, bodies counted; (plus 4–5,000 accounted for by the Yunnan Chinese).

(c)   Most important of all was that every British, Indian, African and Chinese division that had served under XIV Army had met picked Japanese troops in straight bitter fighting and had beaten them. . . . Our troops had proved themselves in battle the superiors of the Japanese; they had seen them run; this was the real and decisive result of these battles. We had smashed forever the legend of the invincibility of the Japanese army. Neither our men nor the Japanese soldier himself believed in it any longer."

By 20 July the whole of 80 Brigade was back in Wanjing, in the same rest area that we had occupied before the Iril Valley operation. We were to stay based in this village on the Imphal Plain for the next three months. During this period every man in the Brigade took at least four weeks' leave in India and the remaining time spent in the rest area was taken up by complete refurbishing with new equipment where necessary and the receipt of reinforcements to bring all units up to strength again. Some Brigades in 4 Corps were taken out of the Imphal area completely for refit and rest in India but there was much clearing up to do and we were one of the Brigades chosen to remain in the area. During this three-month period "out of the line" the 11th East African Division was brought into the war in the Far East for the first time. They were given the task of following up the retreating enemy as soon as Imphal had been relieved and retraced our steps down to Tamu where, for us, the whole battle had begun. Once Tamu had been retaken by the East Africans, they advanced to Sittang on the western bank of the River Chindwin and also entered the Kabaw Valley. The advance down the Kabaw towards the south had, as primary objective, the retaking of Kalemyo, a small village at the meeting point of the track from Tiddim eastward through the "stockades", the route from Kalewa on the Chindwin and the Kabaw Valley track. Their ultimate objective was to take Kalewa which, before the war, had been a major river steamer station on the banks of the Chindwin and was the selected and ideal crossing point for the establishment of a bridgehead on the eastern bank of the river. This was to be used as the starting point for the main advance back into Burma from this area.

Chapter 6

THE BEGINNING OF THE END
SHWEBO – KYAUKMYAUNG – YENATHA

During September and October 1944 the 11th East African Division pushed on southwards, sometimes meeting stiff resistance from the retreating Japanese. By mid-November they had reached Kalemyo and by early December Kalewa was once again in Allied hands. This town on the river bank was in ruins as a result of sustained attacks by the RAF in support of the East African advance.

While all this was going on, we in 80 Brigade, still based at Wanjing, had been taking our leave and getting ourselves ready for the next phase of the war. The Brigade now included many new faces as large numbers of reinforcements had arrived. With the opening of the Manipur road to the railhead at Dimapur at the end of the Imphal battles, it had been possible to provide the Brigade with new transport and the Brigade Signals Section had been completely re-equipped with new jeeps. At last the break was over and in late November we were ordered to move down the track to Tamu and into the Kabaw Valley in the footsteps of 11th East African Division. By this time the whole area was clear of the enemy on this side of the River Chindwin and we were able to move down the Kabaw Valley from north to south in easy stages and without contact with the enemy. The first major staging point after Tamu was at Htinzin, which stood on the banks of a large chaung. Here we waited for two or three days before continuing our journey and the only incident of consequence was the field court martial of three Sikhs for rape of some unfortunate Burmese villager from this place. The Brigade moved on to Yazayo, where another halt of two days was taken. Although the East Africans had cleared the Kabaw Valley of the enemy, it was still a deadly place, hot, dusty and full of disease. The signs of battle were everywhere and the track was in an appalling state. Engineers were laying tarred hessian mesh over the rutted earth track, so that heavier vehicles could follow us, but we passed the front of this endeavour between Htinzin and Yazayo and from then on the track was barely jeepable. Eventually we arrived at Kalewa and went into harbour there with orders to prepare for the crossing of the Chindwin. Once we had settled in, we found massive preparations already in hand, particularly by Royal Engineers and "Sappers and Miners" from the Indian Army. A fleet of boats was being built from parts that had been brought up by road from Dimapur and large numbers of rafts were being constructed from wood cut from the local forest. The well-known character "Elephant Bill" was very much in evidence here and his large collection of trained elephants did much to speed the gathering and transportation of the heavy timber used for the job. As we prepared ourselves, more and more vehicles arrived carrying pontoons and eventually a pontoon bridge was assembled in the Myittha River, near the confluence with the Chindwin. By this time the 11th East African Division had established a small bridgehead on the eastern bank of the river opposite Kalewa. The pontoon bridge was floated down into the main river and eventually put into position between the west and the east bank to form the longest pontoon bridge ever to be constructed by Army Engineers. It was 1154 feet long and was shortly to take a large part of the 14th Army across this major river barrier.

By this time it was Christmas 1944 and I received a signal from HQ 14th Army promoting me to Captain and instructing me to take over command of 62 Brigade Signal Section of 19 Indian Division. At this stage I had not the remotest idea where they were and, in fact, had not even heard of this Division, which was very new to the Burma war. Early on New Year's Eve I bade farewell to all my friends in 80 Brigade and made my way to a light plane airstrip near Kalewa to climb aboard an Auster two-

128

seater light plane, which took me back to Imphal. By this time Imphal was occupied only by the Rear Army Headquarters of 14th Army and I was obliged to stage in one of the Field Messes amongst the most inhospitable crowd of officers that I had ever met. The fact that it was New Year's Eve made no difference to their hospitality. Nobody offered me a drink and, in fact, most of these unpleasant individuals were unwilling even to have a conversation with me. As a consequence, I retired early to my sleeping bag and next morning was flown across north Burma towards the Chinese frontier, to land during the afternoon on a small airstrip near to the western bank of the River Irrawaddy, north of Shwebo.

By the time I had sorted myself out, having disembarked from the aircraft, it was late afternoon and I waited amongst the trees on the edge of the airstrip for transport which had been promised. Eventually a jeep arrived, driven by a Punjabi Mussulman (PM) from the Brigade Signal Section. During the drive from the airstrip to Headquarters 62 Brigade, this fine soldier gave me the rundown about my new unit. It was a mixed Section, half British and half PM, equipped in similar fashion to 80 Brigade Signal Section, with the usual communications gear and with jeeps and mules as transport. It appeared that my predecessor, a Captain in the Indian Signal Corps, had been sacked by the Brigadier after a failure of communications in the Brigade during the long march across north Burma from the River Chindwin. The driver had plenty to say about the Brigadier and I gained the impression that he had a reputation for "eating Brigade Signal Officers before breakfast". The drive along the jungle tracks took over three hours and I was glad to have another PM as escort sitting behind me in the jeep with his SMG across his knees. We arrived at the Brigade location in darkness, were challenged and entered the perimeter. There I found my new OC 3 Squadron who was to be my boss at Divisional Headquarters (a position which meant little as I saw him only two or three times in the next few months). His name was Arthur Burrows and he was looking after the Brigade Signal Section until I arrived, my predecessor having left a week before. He got down to business immediately and within fifteen minutes had handed the unit over to me and had left in his jeep for

Divisional Headquarters. I was very tired by this time and decided to do no more that evening, for I was sure that Arthur Burrows had left things in good order before his hasty departure. As a consequence, I got into my sleeping bag and determined to find out all I could about my new job and get down to work early next morning.

I was up early and met the Brigadier at breakfast. His name was Morris and I soon learnt that he had commanded Morris Force of the second Wingate expedition as a Lieutenant Colonel and before promotion to command of the Brigade. He gave me a long talk about the inadequacies of previous Signal Officers and made it quite clear that he hoped I would be an improvement and, if I was not, we would soon part company, as had been the case with my predecessor. With these threats ringing in my ears I left Brigadier Morris and returned to the Brigade Signal Section bivouac area to meet all those British and Indian soldiers who were to serve under my command. The British element was a typical mix of the regular and citizen soldier of the wartime Army. The Section Sergeant made a great impression on me and my later experience of the quality of the man confirmed this first impression. I had not served before with PMs as a complete unit and was to find that they were excellent soldiers who responded well to good leadership, although they tended to have an excess of pride and were easily offended if approached in the wrong manner. They were all tall with light brown skins and, whenever possible, wore their pugris in preference to steel helmets. The Section Jemadar, Latif Khan, who was the senior rank of the PMs, was an excellent middle-aged regular soldier who took a paternal interest in me from the moment I took over command of the unit. He must have been twice my age, was constantly respectful in his guidance during my first few weeks when I was finding my way in this new unit and there was no doubt that he helped me greatly in my dealings with a Brigadier who seemed bent on breaking every Signal Officer who came under his command. Having familiarized myself with the men and equipment of the Section, I spent an hour or two with the Brigade Major to obtain for myself a full picture of the tactical situation faced by the Brigade at that time. I was fortunate to have these first two days in the unit to settle into my new job without the complication of immediate action, for the Brigade was in harbour awaiting a move forward to the banks of the River Irrawaddy.

19 Indian Division had first seen action in Burma only two months before my arrival. The Division had been moved from India through Imphal and had made an extremely difficult march over 500 miles of north Burma to reach its present position near Shwebo. The Division had brought with it all its field artillery and transport and I was told that one of the biggest problems of this long march had been the conversion of foot-paths and rough tracks through the jungle into a state suitable for wheeled transport. Knowing the country over which they had passed from my experiences in 1943, I was amazed that the entire Division had managed the journey, for there were two mountain ranges to cross and a multitude of obstacles which included swamps, teak forests and the thickest type of bamboo jungle.

The next day, while we were still in harbour, I made a short visit to Divisional Headquarters to introduce myself to the Commanding Officer of Divisional Signals, to discuss with Arthur Burrows a few shortages I had found, to ask for suitable replacements and also to introduce myself to other officers in the Divisional Signals. During this visit, I was informed that I had been granted a permanent regular commission in Royal Signals, following recommendation by Brigadier Sam Greaves and Major General Gracey (GOC 20 Indian Division) as a result of my "performance" during the Imphal battles. (Prior to this I had held a wartime "Emergency Commission".) As things turned out, this was the first and last time I was able to visit the Divisional Headquarters of 19 Division because the Brigade spent the following months well separated from the rest of the Division and very much involved with the forthcoming battle. Even though 19 Division had only been in action for a short time, their arrival in the valley of the Irrawaddy had been much publicized in the world press and newspapers had given us the name "19 (Dagger) Division". The Divisional Commander was becoming well-known, not only as Major General Pete Rees, but as the "Pocket Napoleon" of the Burma war. When I read these accounts I hoped that this new Division would live up to the

131

reputation it seemed to have been given in advance of the battles to come.

Shortly after my return to 62 Brigade from my brief visit to Divisional Headquarters, I was called to an 'O' Group at Brigade Headquarters. At this meeting it became clear that the Brigade would soon be in action again. We were to advance to the banks of the Irrawaddy opposite the small village of Kyaukmyaung, which had been a minor stopping place for river steamers on the east bank at this point. Having secured the west bank opposite this village and cleared the area of the enemy, the main task of establishing a bridgehead across the river at Kyaukmyaung would be undertaken. If successful, this bridgehead was to be the springboard for the development of the offensive down the eastern bank of the river towards the south and Mandalay.

At this point in the long war in Burma, the Japanese were in retreat for the first time, following the overwhelming defeat they had suffered at Imphal and Kohima. The Indian and British infantry divisions of 14th Army were forcing them to withdraw from north and north-west Burma towards the south and south-east. Slim's plan was to use 19 Indian Division as a left hook across the Irrawaddy River and southwards towards Mandalay, giving the impression that this was his main effort, at Corps strength. In fact, his right hook moving secretly southwards down the west bank of the River Chindwin and then crossing the Irrawaddy south of its confluence with the Chindwin, was to be the main effort. This force would then move east on Meiktila, thus closing the door behind the Japanese forces holding Mandalay and those facing north along the southern banks of the Irrawaddy between Mandalay and the confluence with the Chindwin.

19 Indian Division, having established a bridgehead across the Irrawaddy at Kyaukmyaung, was to break out, with as much publicity and panache as possible, and press south towards Mandalay and Maymyo. This was to attract as much of the available Japanese artillery and defensive forces as possible, so as to give the right hook on Meiktila the best chance of being successful. As a consequence, the brigades of 19 Indian Division were faced with a daunting task and had some very tough fighting ahead of them.

132

The task began with the clearance from the west bank of the River Irrawaddy of all Japanese "stay behind" parties, left by the enemy on a suicide mission to give us as much trouble as possible, in the area opposite the proposed bridgehead at Kyaukmyaung. This job of clearing the ground between Shwebo and the river took us the best part of a week and all three infantry brigades of the Division were involved. Some stiff fighting was necessary before we were ready to attempt the river crossing.

Kyaukmyaung, which, as already noted, had been a river steamer station for Shwebo in pre-war days, was some 40 miles north of Mandalay and was chosen as the area for the main bridgehead on the east bank of the river. However, a small bridgehead was put over at battalion strength some 15 miles upstream at Thabeikkyin and other crossings were made up and down the river by small parties, with the object of confusing the enemy. On 11 January 1945 we in 62 Brigade made the first attempt at a crossing, using country boats, but this was unsuccessful. The crossing point was then changed and we made a successful crossing on 14 January. We were the first across and a bridgehead was established and thenceforth slowly expanded. 98 Brigade (Brigadier Jerrard) crossed between 14 and 16 January and established their own bridgehead nearby, against very light opposition. 64 Brigade (Brigadier Bain) was the last of 19 Division to leave the Shwebo area and crossed the river to establish their bridgehead, downstream from Kyaukmyaung, on 16 and 17 January 1945.

Once the Japanese realized what was happening at the river crossing, resistance stiffened and the bridgeheads were subjected to desperate attacks in an attempt to throw us back across the river. The Japanese higher command believed at this stage that this was to be the main thrust by 14th Army and they hurried their 15 Division and 53 Division to the area of the bridgeheads in an endeavour to pinch us out.

In this way I found myself in Kyaukmyaung bridgehead as Brigade Signal Officer of 62 Brigade. We had crossed the river on rafts, powered by outboard motors, which had been constructed and were operated by the Royal Engineers and the Madras Sappers and Miners. I had argued in vain with Brigadier "Jumbo" Morris in an effort to leave our mules behind until they were needed for the breakout from the bridgehead, but he insisted that I took all thirty of them over with us when we first crossed. They swam bravely alongside the rafts and crossed without too much difficulty, although the river was very wide. Sadly, most were killed in the next two or three weeks, during which we were subjected to heavy and continuous shelling in the confined area of the bridgehead.

In my heart, I have never forgiven Jumbo Morris for this unnecessary slaughter of my mules; and since then I have read with interest the words of Shelford Bidwell in his book *The Chindit War*. (Lt Col Morris, 4/9 Gurkha Rifles, was first promoted to Brigadier to take over command of 111 (Chindit) Brigade when Brigadier Joe Lentaigne left to take over command from Wingate (killed in an air crash) as Major General commanding the Chindits; but John Masters, Lentaigne's Brigade Major, took actual command of 111 Brigade at this time, as Morris was then occupied east of the Irrawaddy, and well to the north of Kyaukmyaung, as a Lt Col commanding "MORRIS FORCE". That was earlier in 1944 and he was later posted from the Chindits as a Brigadier to command 62 Brigade of 19th Indian Division). Bidwell wrote (page 187 of *The Chindit War*): "Morris was overbearing, tactless and authoritarian, the last man to be entrusted with the political and military subtleties of clandestine warfare". This, then, was my new Brigadier and, after serving for over a year in action under Brigadier Sam Greaves of 80 Brigade – that fine leader of men for whom I had such profound respect – the contrast now facing me was somewhat shattering. I was to find that Jumbo Morris tried to meddle in my job (and that of everyone else!) instead of just getting on with his own of commanding the Brigade. As a consequence, we were to have many verbal battles in the next few months and I was lucky not to have been placed under open arrest on a number of such occasions. However, I survived this hazard and only left the Brigade after the fall of Mandalay on evacuation as a casualty; but much was to happen before then.

Once established in the Kyaukmyaung bridgehead, we dug deep because of the increasingly intensive shelling as the enemy brought up more and more artillery. The 2nd Welch (commanded by Lt Col 'Bun' Cowey, DSO, OBE) established a forward battalion position some miles inland at a place called Minban Taung, which effectively prevented the Japanese from mounting infantry attacks on the bridgehead perimeter by day in sufficient strength to overcome us as we expanded and built up our defensive positions. However, the Japanese succeeded in passing the Welch position at night and we were subjected to strong infantry attacks as soon as darkness fell each evening. The Welch at Minban Taung, however, were under very heavy attack both by day and by night, and began to take heavy casualties. In the bridgehead, we managed to get four tanks of 254 Tank Brigade over the river in the second week and we were also reinforced by the 11th Sikhs, the Divisional Machine Gun Battalion, which was deployed around the 1500 yard perimeter. After two weeks it became vital to mount an operation from the bridgehead to bring out stretcher-case casualties from the 2nd Welch at Minban Taung. (See Appendix A.)

After three weeks in the bridgehead, we were firmly established and were able to begin the breakout to the south towards Singu. The Japanese began to withdraw and 62 Brigade moved to "Pear Hill", some miles to the south of the original bridgehead location and so-called because of the shape of the feature. The hill dominated the surrounding countryside and was set in the otherwise flat area leading to the east bank of the river. It lay on our line of advance southwards towards Mandalay. Tactical Brigade Headquarters, with 3/6 Rajputana Rifles and 4/6 Gurkha Rifles (2nd Welch were a day behind us, after disengaging themselves from Minban Taung) settled on and around the hill for a brief respite in our fighting advance following the breakout. At least that was the intention but, as soon as darkness fell, the hoped-for respite turned into one of the most bloody little battles I had experienced since Shenam Ridge. The enemy threw everything they had at us throughout the night and some really desperate fighting took place. The noise was unbelievable, with the sounds of explosions, small arms fire, mortars and artillery bombardment combining into a horrific cacophony of noise, which was augmented by the screams and cries of the attacking Japanese. Surprisingly, when dawn came and with it silence, we found that casualties were not as numerous as we had feared. There were many Japanese dead, however, outside the wire of our hastily prepared defences around the hill; and with the dawn we found that the Japanese – those who had survived their attacks – had gone. None of us had slept during that night, as we had been too busy fighting off the Japanese attacks, but the order was to move on to the south towards Mandalay and this we did. Our Divisional Commander, Major General Pete Rees[1], was determined that his Dagger Division would be first into Mandalay and would recapture the city from the Japanese. He pushed us all on remorselessly and, more often than not, was up with the leading infantry. He wore a bush hat and a scarlet scarf around his neck and could hardly have made himself more conspicuous to the enemy. The sight of him urging his soldiers onwards became familiar to us all. He took many personal risks in this way and the opinion was increasingly voiced that Divisional Commanders should not take such risks nor behave in this manner; but there is no doubt about it, he got results and our breakout and advance southwards was incredibly fast and effective. One sad result of these forays to the leading troops was that some of his senior staff officers and others accompanying him were killed, but he himself seemed to lead a charmed life. The Commanding Officer of the Divisional Signals (my CO) was shot dead by a sniper while with him on one of these forays. He was Lt Col Forsyth, a pre-war TA Royal Signals officer, who was a member of the Scottish family of plaid and tartan specialists, which owned the well-known outfitters shop in Princes Street, Edinburgh. He had replaced Lt Col (later Brigadier OBE) A.L. "Flags" Atkinson, who had apparently fallen from favour by the time the Division was approaching Shwebo. The adjutant, Gordon Simpson, left at the same time, moving to 2 Division as the signal officer with a Royal Artillery regiment. After the death of Lt Col Forsyth, his replacement, who did not join the Division until after the fall of Mandalay, was (the then) Lt Col A.M.W. (Mickey) Whistler, who was destined to become Signal Officer-in-chief from 1960 to 1962.

As we moved towards the south, signs of civilization increased. To the east we were overlooked by the Shan Hills and

---

[1] See Appendix B – "the nature of the man".

mountains; to the west was the river, which was more than a mile wide in this area; and in between was a relatively flat stretch of country, with many small villages and increasing cultivation. The countryside was criss-crossed with paths, tracks, roads and occasionally by man-made canals. We joined a main road leading from Singu to Madaya and Mandalay, but, where this road led through a defile, armoured vehicles of 7th Light Cavalry (who were now leading the advance) were held up by a strong Japanese defensive position. General Rees immediately switched our main line of advance to a series of dusty cart tracks which ran to the south between the main road and the river. It was while 62 Brigade was negotiating this new line of advance that I had a particularly unpleasant disagreement with my Brigadier, Jumbo Morris. He insisted that I arranged for field cable to be laid along this route of cart tracks and paths between villages as we advanced. Since everyone was moving at the same time (and with all the speed we could manage), there was no firm, stationary base from which a cable system could function. I told Jumbo that it would be a waste of time and that communications between his TAC HQ and battalions, and back to Div HQ, could only be provided and guaranteed by wireless, as the whole Division was virtually mobile at that time. He was adamant, would not give way and eventually gave me a direct order to have my linemen lay field cable along the route as we advanced. This we did until my entire stock of field cable was laid on the ground, useless and never used. The unfortunate linemen (all PMs and thoroughly loyal) then had to reel in as much as they could and catch us up as we continued the advance. Jumbo never once acknowledged his mistake. In fact, he tried to blame me when later we were short of field cable when it was needed and my line parties were physically exhausted.

Now well on the way to Mandalay, 62 Brigade was suddenly halted in its tracks at a village called Yenatha. We were not to take part in the battle for Mandalay after all. Instead we were to liberate Maymyo, the summer capital of Burma, while the other two Brigades and the rest of the Division were to press on to invest and recapture Mandalay.

Chapter 7

BYE-BYE BANZAI
MAYMYO – MANDALAY – MEDEVAC

A hot march through relatively flat open country, interspersed with some patches of thick jungle, brought us to Yenatha from the river. It was a short march and easier than most, as we followed paths all the way. We were settling down in the village by early afternoon. The whole Brigade concentrated in the area and the three battalions were sited around the outskirts of the village. We in Brigade HQ established ourselves in and near the Dak Bungalow. I organized short cable runs to battalions from the Brigade exchange (our 10 – line UC) and the forward command wireless net was closed down to give operators a rare and no doubt welcome rest. The wireless links (Ops and Adm) with Division HQ, however, were kept open and busy.

The village was in a very dilapidated condition and was completely deserted when we arrived, although signs of recent Japanese occupation were much in evidence. Our noses told us, from the characteristic smell of stale cheese, that the Japs had been here only a short time before. The Dak Bungalow seemed to have been used as a local enemy headquarters and was surrounded by quite an elaborate network of bunkers and trench defences which, after checking for booby-traps, we promptly put to our own use.

Brigadier Morris had left the column in his jeep with a small escort during the march to Yenatha, having been called to Division HQ by wireless. He returned in mid-afternoon and immediately called a conference which was attended by the three battalion commanders and all others concerned, including myself. He told us that we were to have a complete day in Yenatha, to change over to an "all-mule" basis, and that on the following day we were to march south-east into the Shan Hills. Our objective was Maymyo and this operation was to be an encircling movement through hills, hitherto considered impassable, in order to take our objective completely by surprise. Division had found us a Shan guide, recruited by Force 136, who knew this area of the Shan States "like the back of his hand". He would lead us up from the flat country of the river valley, by what were described as "smugglers' tracks" (unmarked on maps) into the hills and onwards to the approaches to Maymyo from the north. "Air supply and mules again," I thought to myself as the plan was unfolded to us, and I began to picture to myself all the difficulties and troubles which were bound to arise in the days that lay before us.

Since breaking out of the bridgehead at Kyaukmyaung, and as the country to the south was more open and with more tracks and roads, we had used jeeps for transport to replace most of the mules we had lost from shelling after the initial river crossing. This part-conversion to motor transport had greatly facilitated the swift advance we had been making up to this point. Now the few jeeps we had with us were to be sent back to Division HQ and would move forward with the rest of the Division as they made their frontal attack on Mandalay. The replacement mules we had already received, to fill some of the gaps caused by the disastrous losses in the bridgehead, were now to be reinforced by the arrival of sufficient animals and S.A.A.Ts (mule leaders) to make us up to our normal full complement of 30.

My 2IC and I, with my Section Sergeant and Jemadar Latif Khan, worked for the rest of that day and well into the evening, reorganizing detachments on an all-mule basis, working out load tables and preparing lists of equipment that we would require from Division to enable us to set out on the forthcoming trek to Maymyo and beyond, carrying all that we would need. I originated and despatched the signal to Division HQ covering our requirements and also got on the blower to my OC 3 (Arthur Burrows) to ask him to keep a watching eye on our needs, to make sure we got all we had asked for. He did a superb job for us and next day, miracle upon miracle, everything we had requested was delivered to us at Yenatha.

We completed this work before nightfall and, having inspected the Section's firing positions at stand-to, I checked up on communications. Finding everything to my satisfaction, I decided to have a bite to eat. We had our meal as night was falling, on the verandah of the Dak Bungalow. We were all too tired to talk much and, after eating our fill, we sat around the verandah looking into the darkness, watching the fireflies and listening to the steady beat of the jungle noises all around us. It was a night of pitch blackness and of steamy heat. Feeling like a smoke, I made my way over to the Brigade Office dugout and climbed down into it. The BM was there alone, studying maps of the route we were to take. We chatted fitfully for a while but I did not want to interrupt him for long as he was putting the finishing touches to the Operation Order for the forthcoming move of the Brigade. As I was taking a last puff at my cigarette, a shot rang out in the distance. We stopped talking and listened. After a short period of extreme quietness, two more shots were heard, followed by another period of deathly silence. A telephone call from 3/6 Raj Rif, the battalion covering the northern approaches to the village, reported movement in the jungle to the northwards and, shortly afterwards, elements of 64 Brigade were identified. Fortunately there were no casualties. 64 Brigade had pushed south from Pinle-In to meet us at Yenatha and were late in arriving. They settled down outside the village for the night and, early next morning, marched out in a southerly direction heading for Madaya and Mandalay. (Brigadier Bain, the Brigade Commander of 64 Brigade, had been sacked a short time before this. It was rumoured that the reason for his dismissal was his "inability to overcome difficulties and get on with the advance" with the speed and determination required by Major General Pete Rees; Brigadier Bain was replaced by Brigadier Flewett, who was now the Brigade Commander of 64 Brigade.)

We spent that day, 6 March 1945, completing our preparations and snatching what little relaxation was available in anticipation of the morrow. The jeeps left for Division HQ, taking with them all excess stores that we would not need, and our replacement equipment, including more mules and some items of saddlery, arrived. We slept that last night in Yenatha with confidence that all was ready and with the satisfaction of a hard day's work behind us.

As dawn was breaking on 7 March 1945 the mules were loaded quietly and efficiently, we gulped down some food and, swinging our packs on to our backs once more, we marched out of Yenatha towards the south-east. One battalion led, followed by a second battalion and TAC Bde HQ, and the third battalion brought up the rear with Main Bde HQ. Rear Bde HQ, in the charge of my second-in-command and with much of our reserves of ammunition, and food and reserve water for both men and animals, was to follow later with a small escort found by the Bde HQ Defence Platoon. This rear HQ element was a mule convoy of considerable size.

We had some forty "marching" miles to cover to reach Maymyo and for the first three days 4/6 Gurkha Rifles were the lead battalion 3/6 Rajputana Rifles with TAC Bde HQ came next and 2 Welch, with Main Bde HQ in company, formed our rear-guard. I moved with the Brigadier as part of TAC Bde HQ. As a general principle, "Column Snake" – the LRPG custom of single file through jungle – was adopted, but as the route became more open and we climbed into the Shan Hills more extensive flank patrolling was undertaken. With a Brigade strength not far short of 3,000 men and with many mules in the columns, the (almost) single file of "Column Snake" meant that the distance between the front and the rear of the complete column of march was several miles.

On this first day an easy march through open jungle brought us after two hours to a small river called the Chaung Magyi, which we forded, lapping up the cool fresh water as we crossed. From this point onwards another two hours of steady marching brought us to the Mandalay Canal, on the banks of which we rested for an hour. It was very pleasant to relax in the shade so near to fresh, clean water and, after unloading and watering the mules, we ate our rations and dozed fitfully until the time came to march again. During this halt we established contact with Division for a short time, but as they were moving southwards towards Mandalay as fast as they could go they were not inclined to pass the time of day on the wireless. We did not adopt wireless silence until we were within two days' march of our objective, but nevertheless wireless transmissions were kept to a minimum throughout the approach march to Maymyo.

We crossed the canal and resumed our march to the southeast, the steady onward plod being interrupted only once each hour when a blast on the whistle signalled the whole column to rest for five minutes. As the afternoon passed, we began to realize that we were entering the foothills of the Shan States. On either side of us hills began to rise and, although the track we followed had only a slight gradient at this stage, it soon became evident that from now on we would be climbing steadily into the mountains. At the same time the country became more wild, with patches of very thick jungle and a deteriorating track which eventually disappeared. From then on we were marching across country. Our Shan guide from Force 136, who was with 4/6 GR at the head of the column, must have known where he was going, but we tried to keep an eye on his navigation by using our compasses and maps. From the latter we were able to identify hill features as we progressed but no paths were marked and, although we were now making a form of track with our marching feet, our Shan guide proved to be worth his weight in gold.

The pace of the march slowed with the difficulties of the country through which we were now passing and we harboured at 1900 hours that evening. By this time we were well up into the foothills. No contact had been made with the enemy and we felt reasonably sure that our detachment from the rest of the Division and our secret approach towards Maymyo had not been detected. Once the mules had been unloaded, rubbed down and fed, the all-round defensive positions sited and manned and wireless communications established briefly with Division HQ, we slept in the jungle where we lay. Sleep came easily, for we were tired after the day's march. The less fortunate on wireless operator and picket duties throughout the night must have had to fight against sleep, but inspection during the night found them alert in spite of their exhaustion.

The next morning, 8 March, we moved out at dawn and found

ourselves marching through more open jungle and climbing steadily. The march routine remained the same, with a brief halt each hour, and we progressed at a steady pace, climbing all the time into the hills. At one halt during the morning a patrol passed us, returning to 3/6 Raj Rif on completion of its task to the southern flank of the column. The patrol was of platoon size and the Rajput soldiers were under the command of a British subaltern. As he went by the spot where I was resting I recognized him as Brian Yates, a charming Anglo-Indian who had been an infantry officer cadet with me at the O.T.S. Bangalore in 1942. We greeted one another and talked briefly. Three years had passed since we had last met and I had had no idea that he was serving with the Rajputana Rifles in 62 Brigade. He was a completely changed man from the youth that I remembered. His manner was jumpy, in fact almost incoherent, and it was evident that his nerves were shot to pieces. I hoped that he would be recommended for MEDEVAC, for I formed the opinion that, in action, he would be a danger not only to himself but also to the soldiers under his command. The life of an infantry subaltern with a battalion in action in Burma was a nerve-wracking experience and all too frequently was very short lived. I have often wondered whether or not Brian Yates survived the rest of the war.

That second night we halted and made our bivouacs an hour before darkness fell. The routines were unchanged but we noticed that it was much cooler during the night than it had been when we were down in the river valley. During that second day we had passed over the first of two high mountain ridges and had now settled down for the night in a slight valley, with another range of hills before us to be tackled on the morrow.

We set off again at dawn on the third day, 9 March, and continued the upward climb at a faster pace, halting only once every two hours for a short break. In the early afternoon we suddenly emerged from the rough country on to a well defined track which ran along a ridge at right angles to our line of approach and stretched away along the ridge to north and south. The column turned to the right and headed south along the track, which evidently led to Maymyo.

We pushed on along this track at increased speed, passing

through a small village on our way. In this village I noticed a hut with a garden in front of it, surrounded by a hedge and with a garden gate in the style of an English garden. Leaning on the gate, watching the column go by, was a man dressed in a loongyi, deeply tanned but obviously not a Shan nor Burmese. I noted that his forearms bore tattoos; one was a heart with an arrow through it and a girl's name. I stopped for a moment to talk to him and it transpired that he was a private soldier from the Cameronians who had escaped during the 1942 retreat. He had settled in the village, had been hidden by the villagers whenever Japanese patrols had passed through, had gone native, married and had one child. He was very lucky to have evaded the Japanese for three years and also fortunate that he had not been betrayed, as the Shans in general were nice gentle people but not as pro-British and anti-Japanese as the Kachins. Perhaps his marriage to a Shan girl of the village had helped. He had virtually become a Shan tribesman, fully accepted in the village. He probably stayed on there for the rest of his life. We moved on, for now our objective was near and preparations for our surprise attack on Maymyo at dawn the next day had to be finalized before darkness overtook us that evening. We could not waste time checking the story of this one-time soldier, nor could we take him into custody as a probable deserter; so we left him and purposefully forgot about him.

Five miles to the north of Maymyo the Brigade halted and deployed, with one battalion on either side of the track we had been following and the third battalion (3/6 Raj Rif) remaining in the area of the track with Brigade HQ and the Signal Section. The Brigade Commander called in the three battalion commanders and those others of us concerned and held a final conference before the attack on Maymyo, which was to take place the next day, 10 March 1945. Reconnaissance patrols from 4/6 GR, taking extreme care not to be seen, had confirmed that the Japanese in the town seemed completely unaware that they were in imminent danger of being attacked by a complete infantry brigade. The garrison in Maymyo consisted mainly of administrative and logistic troops. It was the equivalent of their Rear Army HQ, with such units as Pay, Records and Ordnance stores. There was actually a branch of the Yokohama Bank which they had set up in the town with Japanese civilian staff. There was also a large prison and internment camp, guarded by Korean soldiers and filled with Anglo-Burmese and Anglo-Indian women, as well as a number of British women prisoners who had been caught in the Mandalay and Maymyo area at the time of the 1942 retreat.

Maymyo has the delightful climate of a hill station for most of the year. The cantonment area had many spacious bungalows, set in large gardens. These had been occupied in pre-war days mainly by British government officials and businessmen with their families. Beautiful shrubs and flowers grew in abundance and there were even wild strawberries to be found. Tennis courts and a golf course graced the cantonment area, although when we found them they were much neglected. The summer (hot season) residence, built for the British Governor-General of Burma before the war, was a fine brick house, designed in typical British style and known as Flagstaff House. It was set in a very large garden, with fine lawns (somewhat neglected during the Japanese occupation) and a sweeping tarmac drive leading to the house from the road. Inevitably it had been used as the residence of the most senior Japanese officer during the occupation. In the town itself there was a large bazaar, shopping and business area and many well-built houses for the Burmese and Shan population, but without the lavish provision of gardens to be found in the cantonment area. A railway ran through the town from Mandalay to Lashio on the border with China, with the railway station situated slightly to the north-east of the town centre. A good tarmac road ran down to Mandalay, some 25 miles to the west, and also up to Lashio. (This was part of the old Burma Road which had been used to carry supplies to China until it was cut in 1942 by the Japanese invasion and occupation of Burma.)

At the conference Jumbo Morris gave his orders for the surprise attack on the town, to start at dawn the next morning. 3/6 Raj Rif were to move cross-country around the edge of the town to the north-east, getting into position during the night and, having cut the road and railway leading to Lashio, would move into the town at dawn from their start point astride the Lashio road. 2nd Welch were to take similar action to the south-west, to cut the road and rail leading to Mandalay and move into the town from the west at dawn from their start point on the Mandalay road. 4/6 GR with TAC Bde HQ would move into the town at dawn along the track we had been using for the last stages of the approach march. Main and Rear Bde HQ would remain in the present location until called forward on successful completion of the operation, when Maymyo was in our hands. As ranges were short, control and communication would be by wireless throughout, using voice with our No 22 sets on HF groundwave. Control would be with Main Bde HQ, with TAC Bde HQ and battalion HQs as outstations, as Main HQ would be static until the operation had been completed. In addition, Main HQ would establish and maintain wireless communications with Division HQ (located at this time just north of Mandalay). However, wireless silence on *all* wireless links would continue without exception until the assault had begun at dawn on 10 March.

This was the basis of the plan for the relief of Maymyo and we all left the conference to complete our preparations. The battalions had to reconnoitre routes to their start points and then move to these locations overnight without giving away their presence to the enemy. As a consequence, a great deal of care was necessary and it is to the credit of all in 62 Brigade that the Japanese had no forewarning of the attack. The first they knew of our presence was when we made our first moves at dawn the next day and started to enter the town from three different directions.

During the final conference in the afternoon of 9 March a signal was received from my 2IC (my control set was on listening watch and he broke wireless silence to send the signal). This told us that he had led his Rear Bde HQ column northwards when reaching the track which led to Maymyo, and had marched *away* from us for several hours instead of following us towards the south and our objective. This appalling error of map-reading (or basic sense of direction) meant that the reserves of ammunition and food carried in his column would not be available for us when planned but would arrive many hours late. Brigadier Jumbo Morris was so enraged at this news that he almost had a seizure and tended to try to blame me for the shortcomings of my unfortunate subaltern. The upshot was that my 2IC was ordered by wireless to retrace his steps with his mule column and march southwards all night without stopping, in order to reach us before dawn. This he did and the column arrived, in a state of complete exhaustion, in the early hours of 10 March 1945. As a result, the reserve ammunition and food were available as planned and the Brigadier appeared to be satisfied, for he made no further mention of the incident.

The assault on the town began exactly as planned and surprise was complete. One opportunity was missed by 3/6 Raj Rif in that a fully laden train with steam up and about to leave the railway station for Lashio and the Japanese forces facing the Chinese in the area bordering Yunnan, managed to get away to the north-east before the battalion could stop it. The fighting continued all day and the three battalions slowly took over the whole town. There was little organized resistance, but, as usual, small parties of Japanese fought to the last among the bungalows and in the more densely populated bazaar, shopping and business areas at the town centre. Some bitter street fighting took place in some isolated parts of the town, but by nightfall on 10 March most of Maymyo was in our hands. Later that night a convoy of lorries attempted to escape by the road leading down to Mandalay but 2nd Welch had prepared an ambush on the road to cover just this eventuality and the resulting action gave us some forty-six vehicles in running order. These were put to use as Brigade transport and were a welcome addition to our hard-worked mules. By the morning of 11 March the town was clear of Japanese, apart from one or two small and isolated pockets of resistance, and the Brigade settled down to consolidate our gains and bring some order out of the chaos that inevitably existed after the fighting. Action was also put in hand from both Mandalay and Maymyo to open the road between the two towns so that motor vehicles could get through to us with supplies.

During the advance into the town on 10 March we in TAC Bde HQ had moved with the Gurkhas of 4/6 GR into the centre of the town from the northern outskirts. On our way we came to the Internment Camp for women prisoners. The Korean guards – those who had not been killed by the advancing Gurkhas – had fled and, for the first and only time during my service in Burma, I was present when the inmates of a prison

147

camp were freed. It was an experience I will never forget. These emaciated women awoke that morning to yet another day of brutal imprisonment and found instead, and to their amazement, that we had arrived and their ordeal was over. It is difficult to describe their evident joy, relief and gratitude. There was a great deal to be done for them, including an urgent need for medical attention, provision of food and other administrative arrangements. We were not equipped for this – our purpose in life was hunting and killing Japanese soldiers – and, although we did what we could, adequate arrangements had to come later.

The Brigadier decided to set up his Brigade Headquarters (TAC, Main and Rear) at Flagstaff House. There were actually several bathrooms in this fine building and each one of us, in due course, was able to take the first bath we had had in months. On arrival at Flagstaff House my first task was to position wireless detachments in the grounds of the house and to open communications with Division HQ. Brigadier Jumbo Morris was eager to report, by priority signal, our success in capturing Maymyo. In fact the signal was already enciphered and awaiting transmission. Unfortunately our No 22 sets, being HF equipments, had the usual disadvantages. We were some 25 miles from Division HQ, at this time located in Mandalay. This distance was too far for ground wave and too close for satisfactory skywave working. We were experiencing the problems of "skip distance". As a result, it took a considerable time for me to sort out a workable hand-speed morse link for both Ops and Adm traffic. Jumbo Morris was hovering around, lecturing me about the use of a compass to align my aerials and interfering in general with the work we were doing to get through. I tried to explain the problems of "skip distance" to him but he would have none of it. He became more and more short-tempered but eventually we were through and his message, telling the Divisional Commander that we had taken Maymyo, was passed and acknowledged. Communications to battalions on our forward command net were not a problem as my detachments with all three battalion HQs were within ground-wave range in the area of the town and I was also able to run cable for telephone communications soon after we had settled in. It is of interest to note that, as we had neared Maymyo on 9 March, an OSS agent (a lone white US soldier of unknown rank, dressed in battered jungle fatigues) had appeared from the forest at the side of the track. He had provided the Brigadier and the Brigade Intelligence Officer (BIO) with some very useful information about Japanese dispositions in and around Maymyo. I had a brief chat with him and Jumbo Morris and I examined his pack wireless, powered by a very lightweight cycle generator. It transpired that he worked periodic schedules to his controller in Kunming, some three hundred miles away, by hand-speed morse, using an end-fed aerial. I think it likely the Brigadier reasoned to himself that, if this OSS agent could work wireless schedules over distances of several hundred miles, we should be able to work a mere 25 miles with No 22 sets. I tried to explain to him that our No 22 sets could also communicate HF sky wave over hundreds of miles but, because of the problems of "skip distance", 25 miles could be considerably more difficult. I think he believed that I was trying to baffle him with science and he would not listen.

After a few days in Maymyo – busy days, for there was much to do – we received a signal ordering us to rejoin the rest of the Division in Mandalay. By this time the city had fallen and was clear of the enemy. The order stipulated that one of our battalions was to remain in Maymyo for the time being, to continue with the defence of the town and to establish some order out of the chaos immediately following our recapture of the place. This battalion was to remain in Maymyo until a brigade of 36 (Br) Division – at that time moving south from north-east Burma – arrived to relieve it. The battalion would then move down to the river valley by the main road to rejoin the Brigade.

Meanwhile, at about this time, my body was starting to rebel once more, in much the same way as it had towards the end of the first Wingate expedition, Operation LONGCLOTH, in 1943. Since we were in the middle of the dry season – the best campaigning weather, with the monsoons not due to start until June – the march from the river valley to Maymyo had been hot and dusty but in no way as debilitating as my experiences in the Naga Hills in June/July 1944, during the Iril Valley operation. If we had been called upon to cope with the ceaseless pouring rain, the mud and the abject misery and discomfort of climbing into the hills during the monsoon, the march would have taken very much longer. In fact it would probably have been impossible by the route we had followed. In any event, we would have arrived at Maymyo in a far less ready state for the assault than had now been the case. Nevertheless my body started to tell me that, after almost three years in Burma, I could not take much more. Throughout the march from Yenatha I had the familiar beginnings of dysentery. This was the third time, so I knew the form. I had deep leg ulcers (jungle sores) on both legs below the knees. These often started after leeches had found a food source (my blood) on my shins and calves; in this instance, during marches through wet jungle in the river valley. My height was 6ft 1½" in socks and, in Maymyo, my weight was down to 8 stone. And now, on the move to Mandalay, I collapsed and had to complete the journey on a stretcher. It was later established that I was also suffering from jaundice, exhaustion, a high fever and, to cap it all, acute sinusitis; and the dysentery turned out to be the amoebic variety, so I was a bit of an all-round mess and not much further use to my men nor to the Brigade. I have a vague memory of seeing Arthur Burrows' face looking down at me and greeting me when I came into Mandalay on my stretcher. Soon after that I was lifted into a light aircraft (I believe it was an L-5) and found myself next to another casualty, also on a stretcher. I think the two of us were the maximum stretcher case load for the L-5. We flew from Mandalay to a location near Shwebo, where we landed on a very small strip and were taken to a Casualty Clearing Station (CCS) in tents hidden away in the jungle. I lay there for some days. I cannot remember for how long or much about it. One thing I do remember, though, is that Malcolm Luscombe, a company commander from 1 Devon in my previous home of 80 Brigade (20 Indian Division) and an old friend and comrade from the Shenam battles, was in the next bed to me in this CCS. He was peppered all over his face, chest and legs with small pieces of greyish black plastic from a Japanese grenade. He told me that he had made the classic mistake of approaching the "body" of a Jap officer, because he thought he had seen a slight movement. Inevitably the Jap turned out to be severely wounded but not dead. As Malcolm got near to him, the Jap pulled the pin

150

from his grenade, killed himself and badly injured my friend.

In due course we were moved on stretchers to a larger airstrip and loaded into a C-47 Dakota aircraft which was soon filled with other stretcher cases. There followed a long flight to Dum-Dum Airport near Calcutta, from where I was moved to an Army hospital in Calcutta itself. After several weeks there, about which I can remember little except for the wonderful care and nursing I received and the endless treatment that seemed to be required – my jungle sores were dressed repeatedly each day and I seemed always to be taking tablets, having injections, blood tests and X-rays – I was put on to a hospital train with many others and moved to Base Hospital at Ranchi. There I stayed for the next three months, being nursed back to health. In May 1945, soon after I had been settled in to a ward in the Base Hospital, we heard the wonderful news of the German surrender and the end of the war in Europe. Sadly the brutal war with the Japanese continued, but we knew in our hearts that the campaign in Burma would soon be over.

Towards the end of July 1945 I went before a Medical Board and was granted sick leave for one month. On completion of this leave, I was required to return to Ranchi for a second Medical Board, which could determine my future. I was permitted to take my sick leave where I wished, provided it was in a hill station. Inevitably I elected to return to Kashmir for the third time and to stay with someone who lived in Srinagar and who I had first met on my sick leave after LONGCLOTH in 1943. She had nursed me back to health then and I knew that she would do the same for me again.

The train journey from Ranchi to Calcutta and onwards across the breadth of Northern India to Rawalpindi took the usual long and tedious two days, but the change from the fighting in Burma was bliss. From 'Pindi, I hired a car for the long drive past Murree and over the mountains to the Vale of Kashmir and, at her home in Srinagar close to Dal Lake, she was expecting me. It was as though I had never been away.

*   *   *

The news that the first atomic bomb had been dropped on Hiroshima on 6 August came as a complete and stunning surprise to us. When the Americans followed this by dropping a second bomb on Nagasaki on 9 August, we began to realize the profound effect these weapons might have on the determination of the Japanese people to resist to the end; and then came the news that Japan had surrendered unconditionally on 14 August 1945. At last this terrible war had come to an end. There was cause for celebration all over the civilized world and those of us who were lucky enough to be in Srinagar at the time did our fair share of celebrating. I realized, however, that there would still be a considerable amount of fighting in Burma and Siam, for some Japanese soldiers, deep in the jungle, would not be in communication with the outside world and would not know that the war had ended. Others would never accept the surrender and would go on fighting until they were killed. However, from my own personal and selfish point of view, I now felt reasonably sure that I would not be called upon again to rejoin the fighting in Burma.

During my third week in Srinagar I received an official letter which cancelled my previous orders to return to Ranchi and instructed me, instead, to attend a Medical Board at the BMH in Murree on the day following the end of my sick leave. I was then to proceed to Mhow to await repatriation to the United Kingdom "after long and continuous service overseas". This change of plan delighted me, as it meant that I would not have to leave Kashmir early to allow two days for the long rail journey back to Ranchi. Instead, I could have three more days in Srinagar and then drive down to Murree in time for the Medical Board.

After a somewhat tearful farewell, for we did not know if or when we would see one another again, I hired a car to take me down to Murree. I remember there was a thick mist as we drove into this lovely hill station and there was a chill in the air. I was given a bed for the night in the hospital and attended my Medical Board the next morning. After this I was told that I had been found fit again (category A1) and could return to normal regimental duty. A booking was made by the hospital administration for me to travel by train from Rawalpindi to Mhow and the next day I was driven to the railway station at Rawalpindi in time to join the "Frontier Mail". A normal first class sleeping compartment had been reserved for me and, when I had boarded the train, this comfortable compartment (complete with its own washroom, lavatory, bunk, fan and icebox – what luxury after Burma!) was to be my home for the next two days. The "Frontier Mail" was a well-known express running between Peshawar, near the border with Afghanistan, and Bombay, the large port on the west coast of India. My starting point at Rawalpindi was the next station of any importance down the line from Peshawar. The route then ran through Jhelum, Lahore, Ferozepore and onwards to Delhi, from where it turned to the south and south-west and travelled on through Agra, Jhansi, Bhopal and finally to Khandwa Junction. The "Frontier Mail" went onwards to Bombay but travellers to Mhow had to leave the train at Khandwa and change to the narrow gauge branch line which ran from Khandwa through Mhow to Indore. All those who have been stationed at Mhow are unlikely to have forgotten Khandwa Junction, a most uninteresting place, where one usually had to change from or on to a main line train in the middle of the night.

During this long train journey from Rawalpindi (as with every train journey I made in India), arrival at each station where we stopped was greeted not only by the heat, noise and smells but also by the cries of vendors on the platforms, selling such items as warm ("garm", pronounced "garum") milk ("dudh", as in "good", but elongated into "garum doodh" to catch the attention of possible buyers) or hot tea ("garm chae" – pronounced "garum char-ay"). As one tended to pass the time on these long and tedious journeys either reading or sleeping, each stop tended to be remembered as a rude interruption of sleep or a major distraction from the book being read. However, there was always much of interest during such train journeys and most of the stops provided a fascinating study of the living India of that period.

I arrived at the Signals Training Centre (STC) at Mhow as planned and for the next week or so did little work of any consequence. I was asked to give a few lectures to reinforcements recently arrived from UK, telling them about Burma, to reassure them that life there was not quite as bad as rumour had it. I remember that one of the popular beliefs and anxieties was that mepacrine (the malaria suppressive drug in tablet form that all were compelled to take daily in Burma) was sexually suppressive. This, of course, was nonsense but was widely believed. I was asked to give the new arrivals reassurance on this and I did my best, but whether they believed me or not I will never know.

The staff at the STC treated me well and were extremely helpful to all those who arrived at Mhow having just come out of Burma. I was told that my move to Deolali, to await passage on a troopship back to the UK, might be ordered in three or four weeks' time and that, if I wished to apply for leave in the meantime, this request would be granted, subject to immediate recall by telegram if necessary. Needless to say, I went back to Srinagar for a further three weeks' leave.

By this time it was mid-September and the news was filled with reports of the release of those prisoners of war who had somehow managed to survive the barbarous treatment meted out by their Japanese captors. After I had been back in Kashmir for ten days we were invited to an engagement party, given for a Captain in the Gurkha Rifles who had become engaged to marry a young widow, a close friend of the person with whom I was staying in Srinagar. This young woman, a delightful person, had been married to another officer in the Gurkha Rifles who had been notified as "missing, believed killed" at the beginning of 1942, during the disastrous Malayan Campaign which ended with the fall of Singapore. Two years after receiving the notification that her husband was missing, believed killed, she received confirmation by official letter from GHQ, New Delhi, that her husband was dead. Now, eighteen months later, she had fallen in love and decided to marry again. It was a joyful occasion and the couple received congratulations and presents from all of us. The next day a telegram arrived from Calcutta. It was from her "dead" husband, saying that he had been released from captivity, had been flown in from Siam and would be joining her in Kashmir as soon as the doctors would permit him to travel. I left Srinagar before the resultant dilemma had been resolved. As a consequence, I never knew how this tragic story ended. These were troubled times.

After yet another tearful farewell I returned again to Mhow by the same long train journey, having received a recall telegram in the middle of the third week of my leave. On arrival at the

154

STC I was told that my "PYTHON" repatriation number had come up and that I was to move immediately to the transit camp at Deolali, to await orders to embark on a troopship homeward bound. I travelled back to Khandwa Junction and onwards to Deolali during the next day and then spent the next two or three weeks in the transit camp, feeling bored and impatient, sentiments shared by the others who were waiting there with me. Some of us managed to go down to Bombay for a quick visit to relieve the boredom, but otherwise this was a period so uneventful that little is remembered. In one respect, however, Deolali is of considerable interest. This small town is situated some 150 miles inland from Bombay. In pre-war days and for many years before, it had been notorious as the location of a military psychiatric hospital. It was to this hospital that soldiers of the British Army in India, who were diagnosed as mentally unsound or considered to be suffering from mental illness (who had gone round the bend) were sent for trans-shipment back to the United Kingdom for psychiatric treatment or for invaliding out of the Army. In this way, such expressions as "he is a bit Doolally" or "he has gone Doolally" – meaning that somebody is or has become mentally unsound – is now part of the accepted slang of our language, introduced by British soldiers returning home to Blighty from India. (It is of interest to note that "Blighty" is a corruption of the Urdu word "Wilayati", which means "a country over the sea", and was also no doubt introduced as slang by British soldiers returning from service in India.)

At last the day came when I was moved down to Bombay and boarded the liner *Empress of Scotland* from Ballard Pier. The ship had been named the *Empress of Japan* when she was launched, but the name was changed when hostilities with Japan began in 1941. This time I travelled in a cabin shared with two other officers, a marked contrast to my outward voyage around the Cape in the *Stratheden* in 1941, when I lived, ate and slept in G-5 Port Mess Deck, down in the bowels of the ship. Our route this time was across the Indian Ocean to the Red Sea, through the Suez Canal to the Mediterranean, past Gibraltar into the Atlantic and so onwards to Liverpool and disembarkation.

I had been away for more than four years, attending what some might describe as the University of Life. And, by some extraordinary good fortune, I had survived. I was home in time for Christmas 1945 and had before me a lifetime's career as a regular army officer; but I would never forget the Burma campaign, nor all those friends and comrades-in-arms who had been less fortunate than I.

Appendix I

19th Indian Division
Kyaukmyaung – January 1945
A walk to Minban Taung
(Written a few months after the events described)

Strangely enough I slept for almost four hours that night. The dawn was breaking as I peered out of my bunker and looked around. There was the Irrawaddy, as sluggish as ever, giving the impression of a sleeping river. In fact the whole world seemed strangely peaceful on this particular morning. I thought of the previous night – a bit quieter than usual perhaps. They had made their usual nightly attack on the perimeter, but somehow their efforts had seemed feeble in comparison with previous attempts. After all, this bridgehead was a tough nut for the best Japanese to crack. The perimeter, 1500 yards long, was a semicircle with the river as diameter. The river to our backs – there would be no getting away if one night the Japanese did succeed in over-running us. This confined space held a complete Brigade, together with a Machine Gun Battalion on the perimeter; they would have to be good to get the better of us. And now we had four tanks over the river – the first tanks in the first bridgehead over the Irrawaddy.

I washed quickly in the river, dashing the tepid water over my head. It was going to be hot today. I glanced at my watch, and

157

seeing that it was 6.00 am realized that there was little time to spare. How lucky it was that the Japs only came at night. They did not come by day to attack us at close quarters because of the 2nd Welch, who were 8 miles inland across the only route the Japs could take to attack our bridgehead; so by day they just resorted to lobbing shells at us from a distance; of course at night they could sneak past the Welch positions at Minban Taung in the darkness and give us hell until next morning. They gave the Welch little peace though, day or night, and casualties were mounting. It must be pretty unpleasant out there, I thought.

I heard the tanks' engines start up a little distance away and realized that there was work to be done. The 4/6 Gurkhas were saddling their mules, putting on their fighting kit and gulping some food prior to departure. I had my seven mules loaded in no time, the wireless sets netted to our control set here in the bridge-head, and the men were ready to march. I ran through the orders. One Battalion of Infantry, four tanks, tactical Brigade HQ and my wireless sets; a line to be laid with us as we marched; and there were the stretcher bearers ready to move. Their job, the object of this little operation, was to carry back the casual-ties from the Welch. My line party was standing by, ready to move; I checked with the Sergeant that all my men had three days' rations, made sure we were carrying sufficient W/T batteries to last for three days and, finding nothing at fault, reported to the old man that I was ready to move off. A few minutes later we marched out of the bridgehead and into what was to us an unknown 8 miles of country.

The tanks gave us confidence, somehow. The track was just wide enough for them, with dense jungle on either side, so dense that the column had to keep to the path and was consequently spread out for well over a mile. A dazed Jap came staggering back along the column. He seemed out of his mind, probably after the reception we had given him last night, and was willing enough to be taken back to the bridgehead a prisoner. The thought came to me that we had made a good start anyway. My pack seemed a bit heavy, but no problem. I reflected that if our luck held we would all be back in the bridgehead tonight, perhaps after a day containing nothing more exciting than a 16-mile march in the stifling heat.

158

The column wound its way slowly over the ridge between the river and the Welch positions. A strange quietness hung over the jungle, broken only by the revving engines of the tanks in front as they struggled over a difficult patch of path. At last we topped the ridge, feeling sweaty and hot, and began to make our way downhill into the valley below. The path ran along the side of the ridge, following the direction of the valley and slightly overlooking it. Across the valley we could see another ridge running parallel with ours and slightly higher. Another 4 miles up the valley, where the two ridges met, was the Welch position and in between us and the far ridge was an expanse of water and swamp across which the only possible road was by way of the Welch position. It struck me suddenly that the ridge across the valley must be full of Japs and that our whole column was stretched out in clear view before their gaze, moving slowly and clumsily towards the 2nd Welch. I began to think of artillery observation posts and to realize what a perfect target we presented. I thrust these thoughts aside but could not forget them. When I glanced at the Welch Liaison Officer who was marching at my side I noticed that his face was grim. He must have had similar thoughts to mine. He eased the pack on his back, wiped his sweaty face and looked out over the valley. Then he turned back to me. "We won't get back tonight," he said. Yet now everything was so peaceful. The creaking of the mules' harness, the buzz of some insect, the stifling heat and dust, the smell of sweat, all this seemed to blend with the slumberous silence of the jungle to produce an atmosphere that was far from sudden death.

At last the column was spread out in its entire length along the ridge. From front to rear it was in full view of the other side of the valley. We kept moving slowly, feeling the tension grow and knowing we would be very lucky if we did not strike trouble. Passing through a small group of huts, we came across a few villagers and asked them when they had last seen Japs. Last night several hundreds had passed through, they told us, presumably for their nightly attack on the bridgehead. They had returned in the early morning. We moved onwards, leaving the villagers to crawl back into their foxholes, there to crouch until war had passed them by. They were all, without exception, completely

159

terrified and were very reluctant to leave their holes in the ground even for a moments questioning. They were wise.

I looked with pride at my men and mules. Veterans, all of them, the men knowing full well that anything might happen at any moment, the mules stolid as ever and looking dreamily content under their heavy loads. I have a great respect for mules – a steadier, tougher and braver animal does not exist. These seven were the only survivors of a fine collection which had been the pride of the unit. A mule cannot dig himself in, nor can he wear a steel helmet, and consequently shelling took a pretty heavy toll.

I was thinking about mules when it happened. A dull thud in the distance followed by the whine we all knew so well, and way ahead of us a violent explosion. We knew then that we were in for trouble. That first shell must have landed at the head of the column near the tanks. We kept moving, knowing that to stop would be useless, yet feeling reluctant to get nearer to where the first shell had landed. The second shell seemed nearer and then another gun joined in. The column ahead of us halted; nobody seemed to know why, although we could guess. Then all hell was let loose. Shells began to fall along the whole length of the column. At first they worked slowly towards us, then behind us and then everywhere at once. The dull thud, the terrifying scream and the violent explosion went on with deadly monotony, sometimes near, sometimes far away, and always the thought was passing through our minds that the next one might be too near to be comfortable. Everyone had gone to ground, and the column had stopped; the mules stood around a little perturbed but far from panic stricken. I decided to go forward to see what was happening in front. I told my Sergeant to keep his place in the column and move forward with it, for I knew what chaos would result if we crowded with those in front and a shell landed near. A few hasty words and I was away as fast as I could under the weight of my pack. I was lucky and only had to go to ground twice. As a vivid flash of memory in that run forward, I can remember a mule standing on three legs, shreds of skin hanging where its fourth leg should have been, looking helpless and pitifully scared while the remains of the mule leader lay an inert mass on the ground nearby. I had time to end its agony with a

160

round of .45 and then ran on towards the front of the column.

The first tank had lost its right-hand track and could not move forward, thus blocking the path of those behind. When I arrived a party of men were furiously hacking away the jungle on the side of the path to let the column through. The work was soon complete and we moved onwards, carrying with us the wounded and the loads from dead mules. Meanwhile the disabled tank was taken in tow by its consort. The shelling continued unceasingly but nevertheless the column moved forward without further delay. I allowed my men to catch up with me and with them marched in to the Welch positions three hours after the first shell had landed. Somehow finding friendly faces to greet us, and knowing that our march had ended, made us feel that the worst was over. I checked that all my men had arrived, unloaded the mules and opened wireless communications with the bridgehead. Our line was a failure – no doubt it had been cut in many places by the shelling – but we were soon talking to base by wireless. My mules went to join those of the 2nd Welch and my men dug themselves holes in the ground; and with some tea and hot stew in our bellies we began to think our troubles were nearly over. We could still hear shells landing on the rear of the column, however, and were soon to realize that peace was not for us. As the last man reached the Welch perimeter the enemy ranged on us, and heavy shelling continued throughout the day. Uncomfortable though this was, as we were by this time well under ground casualties compared with those of the morning were light. As dusk was falling a direct hit on a bunker killed one of my wireless operators and totally deafened my Sergeant, but, apart from this unfortunate incident, my section had no other casualties to men. With the mules it was a very different matter. Unprotected from flying fragments and blast, and of necessity confined to a small area inside the perimeter, mules were killed or wounded by almost every shell that landed. When we finally marched out on the return journey next day we left behind us one hundred and forty dead mules inside the Welch perimeter. Of my seven mules only one returned to the bridgehead. The 2nd Welch remained holding their perimeter position for two weeks after we left and throughout that period were forced to live in an atmosphere polluted by the smell of 140 decaying mule corpses which they were unable to remove, an experience which defies description.

Night fell with surprising suddenness and, with the coming of darkness, the shelling slackened to an occasional round every fifteen minutes. I spent the night in a dugout with wireless set and three operators. I can remember now how tired we all were and yet none of us could sleep. It was comforting, somehow, to be in good communication with our base, to sit there in the dugout and smoke and listen to the shells falling outside. I remember feeling bitter when a voice from the other end came over the air and calmly told us to 'increase aerial', with a particularly violent piece of shelling going on outside. The Welch Liaison Officer came in later and together we brewed some tea on the floor of the dugout with the help of a Tommy cooker. The old man came in once or twice to give reports or issue orders over the wireless. He had some of our tea and agreed with us that it had not been a pleasant day. We knew that the next day would probably be worse but didn't voice our thoughts. Eventually I must have dropped off to sleep from sheer exhaustion, to wake occasionally when a shell landed near, or when the duty operator checked communications with base. I would wake up and see him by the light of the tiny operator's lamp speaking into the mike, and then lie back and wonder selfishly how long my luck would last; and would go on wondering about this and that until I was asleep again. The Welch Liaison Officer was restless in his sleep, I remember, and his smoke-begrimed haggard face showed the anxiety we all felt.

And so came morning, and with it another burst of hate from the enemy guns with the realization that here was another day to endure, probably worse than yesterday. The first words I heard at the dawning of this new day were those of my deaf Sergeant reporting that all mules except one were now dead. No shock attached to this; I had expected it. I wondered how I was going to get all my equipment back to the bridgehead. I formulated a plan in my mind. One wireless set and a battery on my only mule, give the cable to the signals officer of the 2nd Welch and load the spare set and what was left on to one of the tanks. It sounded reasonable. Our biggest problem that morning was to find enough stretcher bearers and stretchers to carry the Welch casualties together with all those we had suffered in getting here. In the end there were many more men carrying wounded than defensive troops in the column. We appealed to base for air cover – I remember the code word was "Cow" – and this was granted for an hour or two. It stopped the shelling during that period and enabled us to start the return journey without much trouble. We took leave of the 2nd Welch and set off, led by three tanks – the fourth had to be left behind – and an advance guard of Gurkhas. Picture the scene: a long column of stretcher-borne wounded with defensive troops dispersed along its length – an incredibly clumsy formation, presenting endless opportunities to the Japanese. The enemy did not miss the chance either. Within thirty minutes of leaving the Welch positions rifle and machine-gun fire could be heard at the head of the column. A party of the enemy had evidently slipped in between us and the bridgehead under cover of darkness. They were in the jungle about fifty yards from the path, up on the ridge. One tank and part of the advance guard stayed to deal with them while the rest of the column slipped past. Just before I reached the scene of this little action, I noticed a mule unsaddled and slightly wounded, standing in the jungle unattended. I thought of my own mule and decided that he could not be expected to do all the work of the Section. In a moment a rope was around the stray's neck and he was part of my section. He was a little difficult to manage as we passed the scene of the Jap ambush, for he was obviously shaken and shots were flying all over the place, but we got him past in the end and continued on our way.

It was from this time on that the fanatic outlook of the Jap again displayed itself. The ambush party, seeing the column go by unhindered, proceeded to dog our footsteps at a distance of fifty yards up the slope from the path. In spite of repeated Gurkha bayonet attacks, at which they dispersed into the jungle, the Japanese kept reappearing to fire at us with rifles, to throw grenades and even to yell taunts. When our two hours of air cover ended the shelling started again and several shells landed among these fanatics who were following us; but this did not deter them and they kept up their tactics until a platoon of

163

Gurkhas got behind them and finished them off with their kukris. I remember one fellow who ran down the slope to the road, screaming his head off and waving his rifle, until he was shot on the path. He fell just in front of the tank behind which I was marching, and the tank drove over him to complete the job.

The shelling continued, as slowly the column worked its way up the ridge towards safety. The stretcher bearers were in an unfortunate position, unable as they were to go to ground when a shell screamed near and having to take frequent rests to avoid becoming completely exhausted by such labour in the terrific heat. At long last the end of the column passed over the ridge and out of sight of the enemy. The shelling stopped and, after a swift check up to make sure nobody had been left behind, we opened wireless with base, told them we would soon be in and warned them to be ready for a large number of casualties. Then we closed down, loaded the mule and set off on the last lap for home.

I think everyone was cheerful during that last stage, including the wounded who had without exception behaved wonderfully throughout, as had the men who carried them. We were greeted like long-lost children as we marched through the perimeter of the bridgehead. A mug of hot tea and a wash in the Irrawaddy assumed the proportions of ecstasy.

Appendix II

The Nature of the Man
Major General T.W. (Pete) Rees, C.I.E., DSO, MC
General Officer Commanding 19th Indian Division
1944–45 in Burma

In January 1945 the newly arrived GSO 1 of 19th Indian
Division was Lieutenant Colonel John (known as "Jack")
Masters. During the second Chindit operation in 1944 he had
been Brigade Major of 111 (Chindit) Brigade and later, during
the worst of the fighting of that Brigade, he had been in
command of the Brigade in place of Brigadier Joe Lentaigne, who
had been promoted to Major General to command all the
Chindits, following the death of Wingate. After the withdrawal
of the Chindits from Burma in mid-1944 Masters recuperated in
India and was eventually posted back to Burma as GSO 1 of
19th Indian Division. He arrived to take up his new appointment
in January 1945, as the Division was breaking out of the bridgehead over the Irrawaddy.

This extract from John Master's book *The Road Past
Mandalay* gives a clear picture of his first impressions of Pete
Rees.

Waiting for a plane in Calcutta, a general hailed me – 'Where are
you going, Jack?'

165

'G-1 of 19 Div, sir.'

'H'm. You'll be back in a month. Shall I reserve a room for you at the Bengal Club?'

I asked what he implied. He told me that the commander of the 19th was Pete Rees. He'd fired thirteen G-1s in a year. I had met Pete Rees eight years before, on the North West Frontier, when he was a major and I a lieutenant. He had the reputation, then, of being a ruthless fire-eater. Apparently he had not changed. Thoughtfully I boarded the plane.

At Kalewa the R.A.F. had put up a huge sign – IT'S SAFER BY ROAD. But I flew on to Shwebo and reported to Corps Headquarters. The Corps Commander, Monty Stopford, gave me a cordial handshake and invited me to have a few private words with his Brigadier General Staff. I was beginning to have a curious itchy feeling round my neck, as though it were encircled by a rough surface, possibly hempen.

The B.G.S. said, "Your general's a superb soldier, but we're having difficulty finding out what he's doing. And he doesn't always pay the strict attention to orders that the Corps Commander would wish for. General Pete sometimes seems to think 19 Division must win the war single-handed. You'll see that the situation improves. I'm sure . . .'

The itchy feeling vanished, replaced by a distinct choking sensation. The B.G.S.'s parting "Good luck" sounded sardonic, if not actually diabolical.

I got a jeep and went on east, and came at last to the bank of the Irrawaddy, one hundred miles south of the place where I had crossed it, going in the opposite direction, eleven months earlier. There seemed to be a good many troops about, and boats and DUKWs were busily crossing and recrossing the flood, here about a mile and a half wide. On the far side I heard desultory shelling.

A senior artillery officer came up to me and asked me who I was and where I was going. I told him. His anxious expression deepened. 'See if you can do something,' he cried. 'He's over the other side, with the leading infantry section, as usual. Or perhaps he's decided to keep closer touch with the rest of his division today. In that case he'll be just behind the leading platoon . . . Do you see that sandbank?' He pointed an accusing forefinger.

I saw a low, rather small sandbank on the far side of the river. The artilleryman's voice trembled. 'Do you see all those men and vehicles crowded on to it? Those are *the guns*! The entire

166

divisional artillery, no more than four hundred yards from the front, and the enemy liable to counter-attack at any moment. He insisted they cross over. The C.R.A. (Commander of the division's Royal Artillery, a brigadier) protested. I was there! The C.R.A. said, "Sir, I must remind you that I'm responsible for the artillery of the division." And do you know what *he* said? He said, "Mac, *I'm* responsible for the whole division, including the artillery!" God, I hope you can do something to control him.' He inspected me more carefully, and ended despondently, 'But I don't expect so.'

The condemned man smoked a last cigarette with calm and dignity, and boarded a DUKW. It did not take me long to find the general, for he was five feet two inches high, was wearing a Gurkha hat with a gold general's badge on the front, and a huge red silk scarf. His divisional pennant, a scarlet flag bearing the gold device of a hand thrusting a dagger, fluttered from the top of the radio mast of his jeep. The whole set-up would have been instantly recognisable at a mile on a foggy day. The enemy were about two hundred yards away.

I introduced myself to Major-General T.W. Rees, C.I.E., D.S.O., M.C., late Rajputana Rifles, Indian Army; forty-eight years of age, clean-shaven; always wore a small, kind smile; spoke softly, never swore, never drank, did not smoke. He had won his D.S.O. and M.C. as a young man in the First War, by enormous personal gallantry.

He welcomed me pleasantly; and then told me, his eyes steady on mine but his voice never altering its polite tone, that he had wished to promote his G-2 (Ops) to be G-1 in place of the last incumbent, and had been foolish enough to tell the man he could expect the appointment. But G.H.Q. had overruled him, and posted me. He did not hold it against me, but I had better be aware of the situation.

That was all it needed. Might as well be hanged for a sheep as a lamb. I found the G-2, who was close by, took him aside and told him that I had not asked for this appointment, but now that I had got it I intended to run the General Staff my way, and expected his co-operation. Privately I decided to wait a bit and, if the situation warranted it, to force a showdown which would enable the general to fire whichever one of us he then chose. Relations between a commander and his staff, and within the staff, must be so close that no ill will can be tolerated.

I will not here attempt to go into any detail about the situation, but the reader must know that at this time Slim was driving south, down the centre of Burma, with two Corps, 33 and 4. Of these, our 33rd was aimed at Mandalay. 19 Division had just forced the Irrawaddy crossing and was now on the east bank, the same side as Mandalay, and about forty miles north of the city. The other two divisions of the Corps were advancing south, on the west bank, intending to cross almost opposite Mandalay itself, while we drew the defending Japanese north to attack our bridgehead. But all 33 Corps' operations were designed to draw in as many Japanese troops as possible, for Slim was secretly launching 4 Corps, including an Armoured Brigade of tanks, at the real core of the Japanese position in Burma – Meiktila, 120 miles south of Mandalay.

The country was fairly flat, heavily cultivated, interspersed with irrigation canals, small sluggish streams and many villages embowered in palms, each with its pagoda. Isolated hills, densely jungled and thick with bamboo, rose here and there out of the cultivation. The weather was ideal now, but would soon become very hot and sticky.

For myself, I felt fit and surprisingly healthy. I had not really recovered the weight or the reserves of stamina lost in the Chindit campaign, but a return to action had summoned up nervous energy to replace them. The state of the division also helped. It had only been in action four months, all of triumphant advance and successful attack under General Pete's dashing leadership. It was on a regular supply line and the men looked fit and full of fire, very different from the gallant, ragged, deadbeat scarecrows my Chindits had become when I left Burma. The division consisted of three brigades – 62, 64 and 98, each of one British, one Indian, and one Gurkha battalion, plus the usual reconnaissance, defence, and machine-gun battalions, artillery, engineers, signals, and services. The 4th battalion of my own regiment was in 98 Brigade.

We continued our southward pressure and I settled into my job. I found that the G-2 (Ops) had the Headquarters well organised both for battle and movement. This meant that I could concentrate on my real task, to be the confidant and *alter ego* of the general. For the first week I spent nearly all my time with him.

It was a racking experience. One day, after we had been sniped for an hour or so while standing near a forward platoon position, I asked him with heavy sarcasm whether we shouldn't paint his jeep red too, so that it would show up better where it was parked a few yards behind us. Pete thought it an excellent idea. I only prevented him having it done by pointing out that the fire it would draw would cause casualties to the signals and escort sections who had to follow him wherever he went. Pete was inordinately brave anyway, but his insistence on going far forward, and as conspicuously as possible, was based on memories, and books, about the First War. So much was written, after that holocaust, about generals sending the troops into hopeless battle while they themselves stayed in the rear and, eventually, toddled home to die in bed, so much bitterness generated against the Brass Hat, that young regular officers of that era – who became the generals of 1939–1945 – were usually to be found a good deal farther forward than was strictly necessary. But what they lost in control they gained in the morale and confidence of their troops. Nothing raises morale better than a dead general. Pete did his best.

INDEX

171